"If life has thrown you a curveball and your future feels hard and scary, *Not Part of the Plan* is the book for you. Kristen and Bethany have been there. In these pages, they share their deepest disappointments, heartbreaks, and fears. They are gifted storytellers. You'll laugh. You'll cry. But most of all, you'll appreciate the advice of these wise friends as they teach you how to walk through pain and uncertainty and lead you toward a hope-filled tomorrow."

Mary A. Kassian, author of *Girls Gone Wise in a World Gone Wild*

"What do you do when your 'once upon a time' story doesn't seem to be heading in the direction of 'happily ever after'? In *Not Part of the Plan*, Bethany and Kristen address the struggles we face when life takes unwanted detours and show us through Scripture and experience that our ultimate hope is found in Christ. Even in life's disappointments, we can be completely confident in God's greater plan that is for our good and for His glory."

Gretchen Saffles, author of *The Well-Watered Woman*, founder of Well-Watered Women

"This hidden-behind-a-filter generation urgently needs a dose of reality that points them to the true source of hope. That is why Kristen and Bethany have taken a bold step to open their hearts in a raw and vulnerable way to meet you where you are. Take their hands as they guide you to the right path. Trust me; down the road you will find genuine joy. You'll find Jesus!"

Betsy Gómez, popular author, speaker, and blogger with a passion to help others savor the gospel

"Reading *Not Part of the Plan* challenged me to keep my life with an open hand to God. Kristen and Bethany have a beautiful gift for meshing theological truths with practical encouragement for any girl in any season. If you're looking to find hope in the fact that God's ways are better, this book is for you."

Tara Sun, host of the *Truth Talks with Tara* podcast

"*Not Part of the Plan* is a must-read for girls of all ages who want to understand God's will for their lives. This is another excellent book by Kristen and Bethany, who have a unique way of being authentic and biblical—something our culture desperately needs! You will be refreshed after reading this book and ready to trust God with your story. Highly recommend!"

Julia Jeffress Sadler, author of *Pray Big Things* and host of the *Unapologetic* show

"In a time when self-help books often replace solid biblical teaching, women in today's culture are taught your inner strength can help you become successful or 'manifest' your dreams to reality. The world's standard says the inability to overcome hard times and disappointments is because we did not work hard enough. Bethany and Kristen's book reiterates the truth of God: that He is the ultimate source of strength and our source of purpose and joy in the midst of difficult seasons. This book spoke deeply to a lot of wounds and 'letdowns' I have had over the years and even to difficulties I am currently dealing with. It points to Jesus over and over as our hope and source of contentment. I am so glad I do not have to handle failings or disappointment by trying to fix myself and 'do better' but instead am able to bring all of it to Jesus, the author and perfecter of our faith."

Emma Faye Rudkin, founder of Aid the Silent

"Plans are funny things. They can make us feel like we run the world one minute and then completely break our hearts the next! Kristen and Bethany know what it's like to see their plans fall through and are learning, along with the rest of us, how to entrust the unexpected to a loving God. These sisters will leave you laughing, crying, and falling more in love with Jesus, the One whose plan never fails!"

Naomi Vacaro, founder of Wholehearted Quiet Time

"Kristen and Bethany beautifully remind us that the gospel applies to any and every season of life. A much-needed reminder for women of all ages! Definitely a must-read."

Abby Houston, founder of Melodically Memorizing

*not part
of
the plan*

not part of the plan

TRUSTING GOD WITH THE
TWISTS AND TURNS OF YOUR STORY

KRISTEN CLARK *and* BETHANY BEAL

BakerBooks
a division of Baker Publishing Group
Grand Rapids, Michigan

© 2021 by Kristen Clark and Bethany Beal

Published by Baker Books
a division of Baker Publishing Group
PO Box 6287, Grand Rapids, MI 49516-6287
www.bakerbooks.com

Printed in the United States of America

Library of Congress Cataloging-in-Publication Data
Names: Clark, Kristen, 1987– author. | Beal, Bethany, 1988– author.
Title: Not part of the plan : trusting God with the twists and turns of your story / Kristen Clark and Bethany Beal.
Description: Grand Rapids, Michigan : Baker Books, a division of Baker Publishing Group, [2021] | Includes bibliographical references.
Identifiers: LCCN 2021009312 | ISBN 9780801094729 (paperback) | ISBN 9781540901903 (casebound) | ISBN 9781493432844 (ebook)
Subjects: LCSH: Trust in God—Christianity. | Providence and government of God—Christianity.
Classification: LCC BT135 .C53 2021 | DDC 261/.5—dc23
LC record available at https://lccn.loc.gov/2021009312

Baker Publishing Group publications use paper produced from sustainable forestry practices and post-consumer waste whenever possible.

21 22 23 24 25 26 27   7 6 5 4 3 2 1

CONTENTS

chapter 1

When Dreams Don't Come True

(Bethany) have a confession to make. What I'm about to share with you was once a triple-top-secret, pinky-promise kind of thing. Nobody in my entire family knew about this secret except for my dad, my mom, and Kristen. I'd make you promise not to tell anyone, but the cat is out of the bag. You now have my permission to laugh or cringe. Ready for it? *I bought my dream wedding dress when I was twenty-two years old and completely single.*

No, I'm not kidding.

There are two types of people in this world. Those who thrive on risk, make plans as they go, and live completely outside the box, and then those who want to feel safe, have a plan, and live inside the box. I'm the first type. Kristen is the second. One isn't better than the other. They're just different. This will help you understand my crazy decision a little better.

So, the year was 2011. Ancient, I know. Kristen was engaged to her now-husband, Zack, and we were in full wedding-planning mode. I say "we" because this wedding was a full-blown family affair. With five daughters in our family, you can imagine the ups, downs, tears, and cheers that followed us everywhere. Let's just say we didn't lack estrogen in our house. The highs were high and the lows were low. Our poor dad. Kristen was the first sister to get married, so this was a big deal. As Kristen's maid of honor, I was involved in pretty much every part of the wedding-planning process.

One day, we were out shopping for the perfect wedding dress. If you've ever been wedding dress shopping for yourself or with a friend, you know how it can be. It's not an activity that guarantees smiles or success. It can be stressful. Hard. Tiring. And sometimes downright tearful. There's so much pressure to find your "dream dress" that the whole process can be overwhelming for brides (and their sisters).

It was a little that way for us. We had hit up a few shops with nothing to show for it. Kristen was feeling discouraged. Our mom was trying to cheer her up. And I was trying to compliment everything she tried on. We walked into another shop, hoping for the best. Kristen began trying on dresses again. Our small crew gathered to watch. One by one the dresses went on, then off. After a few rounds, Kristen put on the most gorgeous dress I had ever laid eyes on. She looked like a modern-day Cinderella, fresh off the fairy godmother's wand. The top was filled with sparkles and faux diamonds. The bottom was elegant, full, and flowing with a beautiful chiffon fabric. She looked dreamy.

Unfortunately, when Kristen looked in the mirror, she didn't quite see Cinderella. She thought the dress was lovely, but it wasn't *her*. She must have seen my glowing eyes, because she commented on how this dress looked more like me than her. I nodded my head in agreement.

"You should try it on!" Kristen said with a smile.

I'm not sure what happened inside me, but I lost all touch with reason.

Any normal sister would have kindly declined. But I guess I'm not any normal sister. Call me crazy, but I had never laid eyes on a dress that perfect in my entire life. And remember, I don't do anything inside the box.

I pushed back a little to see if Kristen was serious, and she was. *Okay then*, I thought. *Let's do this thing.* I must have shocked the sales clerk who was attending Kristen by asking if I could try on that same dress after her. Probably not an everyday occurrence. She awkwardly unlocked a new changing room for me, and I excitedly put on the dress.

Now hear me out. When I walked into the store that day with Kristen, I had zero intentions of buying a wedding dress for myself. That was the last thing on my radar. I was completely single. No wedding in sight. But I have no problem with getting my ducks out of line.

The minute I walked out of that room to show Kristen and our mom the dress, they both erupted in small cheers. "It's one hundred percent you!" Kristen said, shaking her head and smiling. "It's like you times a thousand, actually."

I had to agree with her. It was totally me. It fit perfectly too. Before I could talk any sense into myself, a wave of fear washed over me. *What if this dress no longer exists when I get married someday? What if they discontinue it? What if I search for months and months and can't find anything even close to this?*

That fear drove me to make a drastic and totally weird decision. I shared my thoughts with Kristen and our mom, and to my shock, they didn't even attempt to talk me out of it. In fact, Kristen encouraged me to snag the dress now if I truly loved it that much. What a sister.

The sales clerk was completely confused when we asked her to package up this dress for *me*. Imagine the scene: Kristen walks in to find a dress, and I walk out buying one. I'll never forget what the clerk asked me when I checked out. "So, when is your big day, dear?" With clammy hands, I answered her in the most honest way I could muster up: "Ohhh, I'm still working on that." She smiled, and didn't ask more.

As we walked away from that store, a thrilling sensation washed over me. Maybe my wedding day wouldn't be too far off after all. Little did I know that my perfect dress would hang in the back of my closet for many, many years to come. That little secret would remain hidden in the shadows of my life while my dreams to get married went unfulfilled.

As the years stretched on, I wondered when my Prince Charming would come to sweep me off my feet. Kristen was settled into married life and I longed for the same thing. But year after year I found myself still single. Every time I opened my closet and saw that dress hanging there, strategically disguised behind the rest of my clothes, I felt the pain of disappointment. Life wasn't turning out the way I had always imagined. This was not part of the plan—not even close. I had the fairy-tale dress but no handsome prince to go with it.

The Unexpected

When something in life doesn't turn out the way you expected, it can be really hard to accept. But I don't have to tell you that. You know what I'm talking about. Whether you're in your teens, in your twenties, or older, single or married—you've faced unexpected twists and turns in your story too.

Maybe you don't have an unworn wedding dress hanging in the back of your closet, but your parents got divorced when you were young and it left you rattled. Or maybe your boyfriend or fiancé suddenly broke up with you, leaving a painful void in your life. Maybe you received a health diagnosis that you never saw coming. Or maybe you find yourself trapped in a habitual sin, wondering how you'll ever break free. Or maybe you're the woman who looks happy on the outside but feels lonely and miserable on the inside. Maybe you experienced abuse at the hands of someone who should have protected you. (Please see p. 110 regarding abuse.) Or, like me, you thought marriage would come knocking on your door a lot sooner than this.

Whatever it is you're facing now, have faced in the past, or will face in the future, one thing is clear—life is unpredictable. And it's hard. Often disappointing. And most assuredly challenging.

> Whatever it is you're facing *now*, have faced in the *past*, or will face in the *future*, one thing is clear—life is *unpredictable*.

Ask anybody over the age of sixty if their life turned out exactly the way they imagined, and you'll be hard-pressed to find one person who says yes. Life rarely happens the way we plan it.

I (Kristen) came face-to-face with this during the first few years of my marriage. Of course I had faced challenges before, but this was the hardest one by far. Growing up, I had always imagined my future with a handsome husband by my side and a houseful of kiddos running around. Well, I got the handsome husband part, but little did I know how heart-wrenching the next decade would be in the kid department.

As a little girl, I loved playing house. It was one of my all-time favorite games. I'm actually not even sure it can technically be called a game, because there isn't a goal or a winner. You just play make-believe. Did you ever do that? This was long before smartphones and tablets were around. It was just good old-fashioned imagination. Of course, I loved being the mom and bossing my little siblings around. It was my right as the oldest girl. At least that's what I told myself. I'm not sure why it was so fun to play house, but it was. Maybe it was my God-given maternal drive kicking in. Anyway, I loved playing the role of mommy.

When my siblings weren't available to play my games, I would play with my very special baby doll named Kathryn. I loved this baby doll more than anything else. I got her as a birthday gift when I was two years old and still have her to this day. When I was a little girl, Kathryn went with me everywhere. I mean everywhere. Friends' birthday parties, family road trips, camping, reunions, field trips, you name it—Kathryn was in tow. If dolls could talk . . . oh, would she have the stories to tell. I was so attached to this doll that I began praying for God to turn her into a *real* baby. Weird, I know. I'll blame that on the Velveteen Rabbit.

For months, I prayed the same prayer every single night. But every morning, Kathryn looked back at me with those same unblinking blue eyes. Looking back, I'm so glad God didn't answer my prayer. Can you imagine? It would have been a horror movie come to life. Even though my prayers went unanswered, my desire for a real baby never left me.

Like most women, I assumed it would be easy to get pregnant. After Zack and I got married, we were open to having kids whenever it happened. Basically, we weren't preventing. After three years, all I had to hold were the painful memories of two back-to-back miscarriages. My heart felt shattered. What in the world was going on? I came from a long line of fertile women and robust birthers. My mom never had problems getting pregnant. In fact, she birthed nine babies. No epidurals. And six of them were home births. Mic drop. Yeah, she was a modern-day birthing pro. So you can see why I thought it would be easy for me too. But there I was, struggling to get pregnant and apparently unable to carry a pregnancy full term.

I'll share more of my story in the chapters to come, but as I write these words, I've now experienced three devastating miscarriages and many painful years of unexplained infertility in between.

This is not the story I would have written for my life. This is not what I expected. This was not part of the plan.

And before you think I handled those losses and disappointments like a rock star, I didn't. After my third miscarriage, I felt so angry toward God. My heart felt like it had been spiritually whiplashed. I struggled to believe that God was good when all I felt was pain.

The Bible told me that God was gracious and kind, but all I could see were grief and loss. Why would a loving God allow me to get pregnant, only to take away my babies each time? Why would a sovereign God choose to write my story this way? My heart struggled to make peace with this reality.

Life Isn't a Piece of Cake

Maybe you've felt a similar struggle in your heart. It's okay to admit it. You're among friends here. Maybe you've experienced the pain of a miscarriage too, and you're still grieving that loss. Or maybe it's not something quite as big and dramatic. Little losses can be really challenging too. Smaller unknowns can be difficult to handle.

Watching all of your friends move into the next season of life while you don't is hard. Seeing a photo on social media of a party that you weren't invited to is hard. Entering a new job with so many unknowns is hard. Noticing a godly guy who never seems to notice you back is hard.

I have a younger friend who had her heart set on going to a specific college after high school. She worked really hard to get good grades and did whatever she needed to do to qualify for this university. After applying, she waited on pins and needles for the acceptance letter to arrive. This was her dream. She prayed every day about it. But to her shock and disappointment, she didn't get accepted. The school said she wasn't qualified enough. This was devastating for her. She had been working toward this for years. Sure, it might not seem like the biggest deal to you, but to her it was earth-shattering. She wrestled with God in her heart. She felt angry toward Him. Didn't He know how hard she had worked? Why would He allow this?

Or how about one of my other friends who received a health diagnosis that cut her life expectancy in half. *In half.*

Y'all, she's in her twenties. She's fighting for faith every single day. Like many of us, she has the head knowledge about God but is fighting for the heart belief to fully embrace these truths. From a human standpoint, her future is scary. Totally unknown. How does she press on with the weight of such devastating news? How does she trust in a God who allowed such an awful thing to happen?

And then there's my other friend, who met an amazing Christian guy and thought he was the one. He was everything she'd been praying for. Godly. Kind. Handsome. Smart. Funny. Disciplined. But after nine months of dating, his true colors started to show. He wasn't all he was cracked up to be. The facade he was wearing melted away like a popsicle on a hot summer day. She didn't want to face reality. It hurt too much. But she knew it would be foolish to stay in the relationship. With a broken heart and a tear-stained pillow, she decided to end things with him. She didn't feel better afterward but worse. Not only did she lose a good friend, but she also lost her dream of getting married. Her future felt bleak. Plain. Boring. How could she move on and find joy again? How could she trust God again?

These stories and struggles are real and they're hard. Life isn't a piece of cake. You've probably heard the old saying, "You're either coming out of a trial, walking into a trial, or in the middle of a trial." Comforting, right?

So how do we do this thing called life? How do we hold on to our faith and stay anchored in Christ when life doesn't turn out the way we'd planned? How do we find true peace when our emotions feel like a crazy roller coaster? How do we live with hope when our heart aches from unfulfilled longings? How do we embrace God's unique story for us when everyone else seems to be getting exactly what they want?

Twists and Turns

At the end of the day, it's as simple and as complicated as this: either God is 100 percent sovereign and good, or He's not. There's no in-between. God can't be mostly sovereign (which is a fancy word for saying that He is Lord over all). And He can't be mostly good. He's either all or nothing. To be mostly sovereign would mean that God is Lord over only some things in this universe but not others. To be mostly good would mean that God is good at certain times but not others. How would that work? How could God be God? He couldn't. And a real God couldn't function that way.

Bethany and I have found ourselves at the crossroads of this tension many times. As we've each wrestled with our own disappointments, unfulfilled longings, and pain, we've had to stare these questions straight in the eyes. *Is God totally sovereign right now in this really hard moment, or isn't He? Is He actually good in this moment, even though I can't see past the pain I'm feeling?* We're going to talk more about God's goodness in chapter 5.

As you face your own set of twists and turns on the mysterious road of life, you will have to step into this tension too. You can't ignore it. Because here's the reality: what you choose to believe about God in the deepest, darkest corners of your heart will drastically impact the way you respond to all of life. Especially the hard stuff.

There's a tiny little verse in Psalm 138 that has been an anchor for both of us in recent years. It's a little promise that can easily go unnoticed, but it holds the key to all of life's craziness. Here it is:

> The LORD will fulfill his purpose for me;
> your steadfast love, O LORD, endures forever. (v. 8)

This verse gets everything right, where we get most everything wrong. It reminds us that the *Lord* has a plan. That He has a good purpose for our lives. He cares for us. He sees us. He's working in and through us for His glory. His love is steadfast and endures forever. Yes, His purposes might include suffering, pain, and trials, but they're not in vain. They're not random. They're not for nothing. His greatest aim in all of this is to draw us closer to Him and to shape our character to become more like Christ's (James 1:1–4; 2 Cor. 5:9; 1 Cor. 10:31).

He wants to work in our lives through our losses. He wants to deepen our faith through our grief. He wants to show us His love and comfort through our unfulfilled longings. He wants to use our lives as a testimony of His faithfulness. He wants to point our lost and broken world back to the Savior, Jesus Christ. He wants to use our disappointments to push us closer to Him.

> He wants to *use* our disappointments to push us *closer* to Him.

When you look at your life right now, you can't see beyond today. All you can see is what happened in the past and what is happening right now. You don't have the full picture. You don't know what God is doing. As one pastor said, "God will either give us what we ask for in prayer or give us what we would have asked for if we knew everything he knows."[1]

Imagine you're holding up a straw and trying to look through it. How much would you be able to see? Not much. That's your view of life. How much does God see? Everything. But instead of trusting the all-knowing God, we tend to look through that tiny straw opening and declare that God is unloving, unkind, and unfaithful. Funny, isn't it?

But here's the reality: The more you get to know God's character, the more confident you will be to trust Him with your unknown future. The more you discover that your life isn't about getting what you want but about walking in an intimate relationship with your Creator, the more you will discover true joy.

Sure, it's tempting to run away from our pain and disappointment when life gets hard. You don't have to tell me twice where the dark chocolate is when I'm sad. And let's be honest: we've all hidden in our rooms with a carton of ice cream in hand while our favorite show distracted us from our pain. (Ummm, guilty.) Yeah, it feels really good in the moment. But all it does is make our middle region a little squishier and our emotional pain a few hours delayed. God wants so much more for us than that.

Hang with us, sis. Don't lose heart. Don't get stuck in that moment of seeing your unworn wedding dress hanging in the back of your closet or never seeing that positive pregnancy test. Look beyond the pain of that moment. The valleys are real and they're hard, but there's so much more God is doing.

Let's learn how to see life through a lens of hope.

Whether you're new in your faith, are a church pew-warming regular, or are still skeptical about God altogether, this book is for you. Join us on a real and raw journey as we share the nitty-gritty places of our lives with you and show you what God has done. We're just regular girls. Texans, in fact. But we've seen God do a mighty work in our hearts, and we can't wait to share it with you. Come laugh with us and cry with us as we uncover these life-changing truths together. Life is unexpected. We need grace for this journey. But more than anything, we need gospel hope.

Let's discover together what it means to thrive in this life, no matter where the journey takes us.

Ponder IT

> The more you get to know God's character,
> the more confident you will be to trust
> Him with your unknown future.

Remember

★ Life is hard and unpredictable, and you can't control the future.

★ What you choose to believe about God in the deepest, darkest corners of your heart will drastically impact the way you respond to all of life.

★ God has a purpose for your life, and His love is stead-fast (Ps. 138:8).

★ God wants to use your trials, disappointments, long-ings, and pain to draw you into a deeper, more satisfy-ing relationship with Him.

★ The valleys are real and they're hard, but there's so much more God is doing.

SHARE YOUR HEART

Dear Lord,

I confess that my faith is small and weak sometimes. When I face disappointments and struggles, I'm not as quick as I should be to take these burdens to You in prayer. I often worry about them and give in to fear. Help me to believe that You are who You say You are. Help me to trust in Your character, even when I can't see You working. Grow me in my understanding of Your love. I don't want to love You when life is easy, then reject You when life is hard. I want to faithfully serve You no matter what happens in my life. Please help me. I can't do this without You. As I read this book, I pray that You'll use it to powerfully work in my life! I want to know You more.

Amen.

Consider

──────── **Psalm 138** ────────

I give you thanks, O LORD, with my whole heart;
    before the gods I sing your praise;
I bow down toward your holy temple
    and give thanks to your name for your steadfast love and
      your faithfulness,
    for you have exalted above all things
    your name and your word.
On the day I called, you answered me;
    my strength of soul you increased.

All the kings of the earth shall give you thanks, O LORD,
    for they have heard the words of your mouth,
and they shall sing of the ways of the LORD,
    for great is the glory of the LORD.
For though the LORD is high, he regards the lowly,
    but the haughty he knows from afar.

Though I walk in the midst of trouble,
    you preserve my life;
you stretch out your hand against the wrath of my enemies,
    and your right hand delivers me.
The LORD will fulfill his purpose for me;
    your steadfast love, O LORD, endures forever.
    Do not forsake the work of your hands.

1 Corinthians 10:31
2 Corinthians 5:9
James 1:1-4

WHAT **ABOUT YOU?**

1. Do you have a "wedding dress purchase" story from your past?

2. What unexpected twists and turns has your life taken?

3. Do you tend to turn away from God or toward God when you face disappointment? Describe what this looks like.

4. How does Psalm 138:8 encourage your heart?

5. What's one area you hope to grow in by reading this book?

Go **FOR IT**   As you begin your journey through the pages of this book, we pray God uses it to breathe life and hope back into your veins. Take a moment right now to write your own prayer to God. Make it deeply personal. Don't hold anything back. Pour out your heart, and ask Him to do a work in your life like never before. Be specific in your wording, and ask God to strengthen your faith in particular areas. Remember, He loves you and cares deeply for you. He wants to hear your prayers.

The LORD will fulfill his *purpose* for me; your steadfast *love*, O LORD, endures forever.

Psalm 138:8

chapter 2

This Isn't What I Wanted

Who in the world would go backpacking on their honeymoon?

Call me crazy, but that's exactly what Zack and I (Kristen) did. Okay, full disclosure: the only reason I even agreed to this painful outdoor adventure was because our honeymoon was six weeks long. Yes, six weeks. I know what you're thinking. *Who in the world goes on a six-week honeymoon?* Sure, it was a bit extra. I have no idea how we managed this with our newlywed budget, but somehow we made it work. We spent the first half of our romantic getaway tanning on the beaches of Costa Rica and the second half snuggling in the mountains of Colorado. It felt like a dream.

Until we went backpacking.

This part of the honeymoon was anything but romantic. We strapped on our massive backpacks (I didn't know they made them this large) and headed into the Colorado wilderness for four nights. Four nights, y'all.

If you want to put your marriage to the test right off the bat, go backpacking.

The trip started out wonderfully. We hiked hand in hand. We stopped for water breaks and enjoyed amazing views. We snuggled in our miniature two-person tent under the stars. It was dreamy.

Then we hit day three.

My feet started to blister. I was sick of eating granola bars. That sweet little two-person tent felt like a tiny torture chamber. My backpack seemed to be gaining weight. My legs hurt. I hadn't taken a shower since we left. I was sweaty, tired, and wondering why in the world I left those beaches in Costa Rica.

Stopping wasn't an option though.

There was no turning back. We had to press on. Did I mention I was still wearing the same underwear from day one?

With the sun shining down, we set off on another torturous—I mean glorious—day of hiking. I was doing okay, until we hit the big mountain. The trail seemed to go straight up to high heaven. The sight of this incline caused my blisters to ache and my emotions to break.

Don't be a wimp, I told myself. *Pull it together.*

My little pep talk gave me enough resolve to keep walking. With a smile on my face, I followed my new husband up the mountain.

After hiking for several hours, I could finally see the peak in the distance. *You're almost there! Keep going!* With one foot in front of the other, I willed myself to keep moving. But when I reached the top, the mountain played a cruel and mean trick on me. *It wasn't the top.* Not even close. It was a false peak.

If you know anything about hiking mountains, you know that false peaks are a real thing. The top looks like it's within reach, only to keep going up on the backside. It's a dirty mountain trick. And that's exactly what happened to me on this memorable day.

Just when I thought the hike was over, it was really only beginning. My emotional resolve was waning fast. My nerves were running thin. But I was too prideful to give up. I didn't want Zack to think I was the biggest wimp on the planet.

To my utter dismay, this false-peak situation became somewhat of a routine for us. It happened over and over again. The real peak seemed impossible to reach. I wasn't sure how much more I could take. My irritation levels were rising. I hadn't worn makeup in days. My face was sunburned and crusty. And that nasty granola bar felt like dry sand in my teeth. My new husband was about to witness a crazy lady. *For better or for worse, right?* At least our wedding vows were probably fresh in his mind. *If I see one more false peak, I'm going to drop-kick the nearest squirrel!*

But no. I couldn't turn into a crazy lady yet. We were barely married. I had to persevere. I had to keep going. With sweat dripping down my back, I put one foot in front of the other. On and on, the false peaks taunted me.

I Just Want What I Want

Real life is full of false peaks. As we journey through the days, weeks, and months of our lives, we're constantly striving toward our goals, right?

We have dreams.

Hopes.

Prayers.

Longings.

Plans.

And just when we think we're getting close to the top, we find out how far away we truly are.

The months following my second miscarriage felt exactly like this. I had experienced the joy of getting that positive pregnancy test and longed to see those two lines again. For me, this was my peak. I wanted to be a mom so badly. Even though it had taken me two years to get pregnant the first time and six months the second time, I didn't think anything was seriously wrong. I just thought it took me longer than most women. I assumed it would happen again soon.

I purchased a bulk pack of pregnancy tests online and kept them hidden in the back of my bathroom drawer. With each new month, I excitedly pulled out a test hoping it would end my waiting. But each month, all I saw was one lonely line. Month after month, I faced the disappointment of my unfulfilled longings. I prayed fervently day after day, hoping the end was in sight. But all I encountered were false peaks.

I was beginning to feel bone weary. Emotionally exhausted. Spiritually blistered. The ups and downs were a lot to handle. I cried every time. Just when I thought the peak was in view, it wasn't. The pregnancy tests were leaving me feeling more discouraged and hopeless each time I took one.

I decided to put them away and just let my period tell me the news. This helped. A little. But each month my heart still ached. I cried out to God to answer my prayers. But all I heard was silence. I was tired of this path; I just wanted to be done. Little did I know that my journey with infertility was only beginning. My longings to see a positive pregnancy test would remain unfulfilled for the next five years. This journey would become one of the most strenuous spiritual hikes I had ever taken.

Unfulfilled longings are hard to deal with. Like really hard. I don't know about you, but *waiting* is a major challenge for me. Having patience is like pulling teeth. I'm a go-getter. When I've made up my mind that I want something, I just want it. *Ummm . . . what's the problem, God? I'm ready for this now!* So when my longings don't become a reality, there's a major conflict in my heart. It's a battle of interests. My plan versus God's plan. Since I often think I know better than God, I wrestle with His timing. *God, could You move a little faster?*

You know what I'm talking about.

I have no doubt in my mind that you've wrestled with your own unfulfilled longings too. Like me, you've poured out your heart to God in prayer. You've been on your own never-ending uphill hike. And just when you thought the wait was over, you were hit with another false peak.

Just today, I got a message from a girl on social media who shared this:

> I am still not married and it's what I've desired and dreamed of since I was twelve years old. If it's not God's will, I have been diligently praying that He would take away this desire, but He hasn't.

What unfulfilled longings are weighing on your heart right now?

Getting married?

Having one real and true friend?

Having parents who genuinely love each other?

Having a husband who leads spiritually?

Living in a city with a bigger Christian community?

Getting a better job?

Feeling deeply loved by someone?

Having nicer siblings?

Overcoming a chronic illness?

Seeing a friend or family member come to know Christ?

Getting pregnant?

Having another child?

Something else? _____

As I've wrestled with my own unfulfilled longings to get pregnant, I've asked God "why" so many times. I've cried and wondered why God would give this good gift to other women but not to me. I've prayed fervently and sincerely and wondered why God wasn't answering my prayers. Why wasn't He giving me what I so desperately wanted—especially something that He calls a good thing.

Maybe you've tried to bargain with God like I have.

Okay, God—if You answer this prayer, I promise I'll read my Bible for this entire year and never miss a day. Think of how much I'll grow!

God, if You give me what I want (and BTW, You call this thing a blessing in the Bible—just FYI), I promise to never complain about anything ever again! For real! Cross my heart, hope to die.

Seriously, God, I'll be a better Christian if I get this. Not even kidding. Feel free to take something else out of my life, but please (with a cherry on top) could You just answer this prayer? And like maybe soon?

There's that moment when we all feel desperate. We're done waiting, and we just want what we want. Bargaining with God is tempting (and I've been there!), but it never really works out in the end.

Here's the deal: I used to think that God wasn't answering my prayers when I didn't get pregnant, but the reality was, He was answering them all along. He just wasn't giving me the answer I wanted. It took me a while to catch on, but I eventually realized that God answers my prayers in one of three ways:

1. He says "yes" and gives me what I prayed for.
2. He says "no" and closes the door in that area.
3. He says "wait" and wants me to patiently wait for an answer down the road.

Out of those three options, I think the hardest one is "wait." It makes me feel like I'm a contestant on a game show with three mystery boxes to uncover. When I uncover the box that says "wait," I think to myself, *Can I try a different box, please? This isn't the mystery prize I was hoping for!* A "yes" or a "no" is a little more straightforward. A little more black and white. I can live with that. But "wait"? That's like living in national fuzzy land. No thanks, God.

But here's the truth: God knows the waiting is hard for us as humans. He knows it's challenging for us. Ultimately, though, He knows it's good for us. The waiting causes us to come face-to-face with our own inability to do anything about it. The waiting forces us to look in the mirror and acknowledge that we're not in control. As a recovering control freak, this isn't fun for me. But it's oh so good for me. God knows that my greatest need isn't to get what I want out of life but to get more God into my life. And if I'm totally honest with myself, one of the best ways for me to see my need for Him is through the lens of my unfulfilled longings. As my friend Nancy Wolgemuth often says, "Anything that makes me need God is a blessing."[1] That'll preach.

> The *waiting* forces us to look in the mirror and acknowledge that we're not in *control.*

Waiting Is the Hardest Part

Not long ago, I met with my mentor and shared with her my struggle of waiting on God's timing. I asked her advice on how to deal with my unfulfilled longings when all God seems to be saying is "wait." By the way, having an older, wiser godly woman pour into your life on a regular basis is one of the best decisions you could ever make. If you've followed Girl Defined Ministries for any length of time, you know we're passionate about mentorship. Having a godly woman in your life you can share your guts with and get biblical counsel from is life-changing. Sometimes my mentor just needs to give me some gentle encouragement and prayer, and other times she needs to tell me to put my big-girl panties on and just do what I know is right. Either way, it's always helpful.

This particular day was somewhere in between a gentle hug and big-girl panties.

I shared my heart with her and asked for her advice. She opened her Bible and wisely told me to check out Hebrews 11. As I flipped through the pages of the New Testament, I eventually landed on the book of Hebrews. (It's always a little nerve-racking trying to quickly find a specific book of the Bible in front of your mentor! Why do I suddenly forget where everything is in the Bible?) As soon as I got to chapter 11, I saw the heading that said, "By Faith." Hmmm . . . seemed fitting. My mentor told me to glance through this chapter and see how many times I saw the words *by faith*. I began scanning the pages. *One, two, three, four . . . a dozen . . . two dozen!* Those two little words popped up again and again in this one chapter. My mentor told me to check out verses 1–3 to get the context for this chapter. They say,

Now *faith* is the assurance of things hoped for, the conviction of things not seen. For by it the people of old received their commendation. *By faith* we understand that the universe was created by the word of God, so that what is seen was not made out of things that are visible. (emphasis added)

Okay . . . what? If you have your Bible handy (or an app on your phone), grab it and turn to Hebrews 11 with me really quickly. I promise it will be worth it. I'll wait for you.

Got it?

I'm serious. This will be so much better if you can *see* what I'm about to share.

Okay, let's go.

What I discovered in this passage was mind-blowing and extremely encouraging to me. As you glance through this chapter, what do you see? You're probably seeing those two little words *by faith* written multiple times. And did you notice how they're always followed by a person's name? For example, let's look at verse 7 together:

> *By faith* Noah, being warned by God concerning events as yet unseen, in reverent fear constructed an ark for the saving of his household. By this he condemned the world and became an heir of the righteousness that comes *by faith*. (emphasis added)

Remember the story of Noah and the ark from Genesis 5–10? God called him to do something crazy (build a massive ark to save his family from a worldwide flood that God promised was coming). Noah had never seen a worldwide flood before. Nobody had. But he trusted God and *by faith* built a massive boat (which some say took him one hundred years). God didn't tell Noah every detail of what was to come. Noah had to trust God and obey him simply *by faith*.

If you glance through the rest of Hebrews 11, you'll see name after name of Old Testament people who chose to obey God by faith without having a lot of details.

> **BY FAITH** Abraham obeyed when he was called to go out to a place that he was to receive as an inheritance. (v. 8)

BY FAITH Sarah herself received power to conceive, even when she was past the [childbearing] age, since she considered him faithful who had promised. (v. 11)

BY FAITH Moses, when he was grown up, refused to be called the son of Pharaoh's daughter, choosing rather to be mistreated with the people of God than to enjoy the fleeting pleasures of sin. (vv. 24–25)

BY FAITH Rahab the prostitute did not perish with those who were disobedient, because she had given a friendly welcome to [God's chosen people]. (v. 31)

All of these people were ordinary people, just like you and me. They each faced their own unfulfilled longings, fears, and unknowns about the future. They struggled to trust God. They weren't superhumans. Just regular humans fighting for faith. Each one of them had to make the choice to put their faith in God in the midst of uncertainty. They couldn't see the future. They didn't have the end of the story. They weren't sure how life would unfold. But they chose to place their faith in God and not in their circumstances.

And that's exactly what my mentor was encouraging me to do.

She used this powerful chapter to remind me that God cares about my prayers and my unfulfilled longings, but He is calling me to put my ultimate trust in Him. He is calling me to find my hope in Him alone. Yes, my desires are great, but they shouldn't be my greatest desire. She reminded me that my relationship with God is the deepest and truest need of my heart. It's the only thing that can bring genuine satisfaction to my soul. And, sister, it's the only thing that can bring genuine satisfaction to your soul too.

In this life, our greatest aim shouldn't be to get what we want but to know God more fully and to love Him more deeply. And we do this *by faith*.

By faith we trust that His timing is better than our own.

By faith we choose to believe that God knows best.

By faith we entrust our future to God and rest in His plan.

By faith we hold on to the promise that if we never get the things we've prayed for, God will still be enough.

After reading Hebrews 11 that day, I wondered how strong my faith truly was. If I had lived during the Bible times, would my name have been used as an example in Hebrews 11?

By faith *Kristen* trusted God to give her the strength to honor Him as she wrestled with infertility and unfulfilled longings.

How's your faith doing right now? What would it look like for your name to be written in the pages of Scripture? Make this sentence personal to you:

BY FAITH _____ obeyed God and trusted Him to provide for her needs as she wrestled with _____

_____.

Enjoy the Journey

How amazing would it be to have unshakable, unwavering, and courageous faith? I want that for myself. I want that for you.

Remember that ridiculously hard backpacking trip I told you about at the beginning of this chapter? The one where I was about to turn into a crazy lady with stinky, three-day-old underwear on? Well, as Zack and I were getting closer to the actual peak, we paused for a quick water break. He must have seen my frenzied state because he turned to me and lovingly said, "Hey, babe, don't forget to enjoy the journey. Getting to the top is only part of the experience."

In that hot and sweaty moment, I wanted to turn to him and sarcastically reply, "Thank you, coach!" but I held my tongue. And good thing. Because Zack was totally right. I had become so fixated on getting to the top that I had forgotten to enjoy the journey. I was missing what was happening all around me. Beautiful views. Fresh pine trees. Cute chipmunks running by.

I was totally missing the journey.

And that's exactly what happens in real life. We get so fixated on our unfulfilled longings that we forget to live life *right now*. We forget to enjoy the journey. We lose sight of the beautiful things that God is doing all around us.

Sis, look around. What is God doing in your life right now? What does He want to teach you today? What has He already given you that you've become blind to? The reality is, if you can't be content with what God has given you today, you probably won't be content with what He'll give you tomorrow. There is so much God wants to do in your life during the *waiting*. There is so much wisdom to be gained in the *wanting*.

One of the biggest lessons God has taught me during my season of unfulfilled longings is that He is enough.

It's not God + My Answered Prayer = Happiness.

It's God + Sincere Faith = Great Joy.

Whatever your journey looks like today, don't forget to look around. Don't waste the waiting. Don't fixate on the peaks. Some of life's greatest lessons happen as we're refined in the valleys.

As I type these words, I still haven't had a healthy pregnancy. And I don't know if I ever will. But that's no longer where my hope lies. That's no longer the peak of my life. I have learned to embrace the journey. By faith, I know that whatever happens in my life, Christ will be enough for me. As a Christian woman, my greatest purpose remains the same: to love God with all my heart and to build His kingdom. And that can happen right now.

I don't know what mountains you're climbing. I don't know what longings you're carrying. But I do know this: by faith, you can choose to put your trust in the one true God who is with you in the midst of your circumstances. Whether or not God ever gives you the longings of your heart, you can find lasting peace and fulfillment in your relationship with Christ.

You'll be encouraged to know that Zack and I did finally make it to the top of the mountain that day. As hard and exhausting as it was, it was worth it. I stood on that peak, sweaty underwear and all, and smiled. Not because the view from the top was so spectacular (although it was), but because the hike itself had taught me the important lesson of looking around and embracing each step of the journey.

Ponder IT

> Whether or not God ever gives you the longings
> of your heart, you can find lasting peace and
> fulfillment in your relationship with Christ.

Remember

- ✶ Your greatest need isn't to get what you want out of life but to get more of God into your life.

- ✶ God cares about your prayers and unfulfilled longings, and He is calling you to put your ultimate trust in Him.

- ✶ Your relationship with God is the deepest and truest need of your heart.

- ✶ As a Christian woman, your greatest purpose remains the same: to love God with all of your heart and to build His kingdom.

- ✶ True joy and hope can be found in Christ right now.

SHARE YOUR HEART

Dear Lord,

You see my heart. You see my inner longings. You know that these desires weigh heavy on my mind. I confess that I want these things so badly sometimes that I lose sight of You. I forget that You're the only One who can truly satisfy me. Please forgive me for chasing after these longings more than I chase after You. Strengthen my faith, like the people who are talked about in Hebrews 11 of Your Word. Help me to trust You—by faith—with these desires and to rest in Your plan. I know that You love me, and I know that You always do what is good. Help me to fully believe that. I want to live a life devoted to You right now, whether I ever get my longings fulfilled or not. I know that true hope is found in my relationship with You. You are enough.

Amen.

Consider

Hebrews 11:1-11

Now faith is the assurance of things hoped for, the conviction of things not seen. For by it the people of old received their commendation. By faith we understand that the universe was created by the word of God, so that what is seen was not made out of things that are visible.

By faith Abel offered to God a more acceptable sacrifice than Cain, through which he was commended as righteous, God commending him by accepting his gifts. And through his faith, though he died, he still speaks. By faith Enoch was taken up so that he should not see death, and he was not found, because God had taken him. Now before he was taken he was commended as having pleased God. And without faith it is impossible to please him, for whoever would draw near to God must believe that he exists and that he rewards those who seek him. By faith Noah, being warned by God concerning events as yet unseen, in reverent fear constructed an ark for the saving of his household. By this he condemned the world and became an heir of the righteousness that comes by faith.

By faith Abraham obeyed when he was called to go out to a place that he was to receive as an inheritance. And he went out, not knowing where he was going. By faith he went to live in the land of promise, as in a foreign land, living in tents with Isaac and Jacob, heirs with him of the same promise. For he was looking forward to the city that has foundations, whose designer and builder is God. By faith Sarah herself received power to conceive, even when she was past the age, since she considered him faithful who had promised. Therefore from one man, and him as good as dead, were born descendants as many as the stars of heaven and as many as the innumerable grains of sand by the seashore.

DIG DEEPER

Romans 5:1-5   Hebrews 11
Romans 8:18-25   James 1:2-4

WHAT ABOUT YOU?

1. Have you ever tried to bargain with God in your prayers? What did that look like?

2. What unfulfilled longings are weighing heavy on your heart right now?

3. What did you find personally encouraging about the faithfulness of those people from Hebrews 11?

4. How has God used your unfulfilled longings to show you your greater need for Christ?

5. As you look at your life right now, what can you thank God for?

Go **FOR IT** Grab a journal or piece of paper and write out (one by one) every single unfulfilled longing in your life right now. Don't overthink it. Just write down each one that comes to mind. Next, write down these words in tiny print right above each one: "God, strengthen my faith to entrust You with . . ." Now take a moment to pray each line back to God. Do this every time you begin to feel anxious about any one of those things.

Now *faith* is the assurance of things hoped for, the *conviction* of things not seen.

Hebrews 11:1

chapter 3

Worry, Worry, Worry

(Bethany) glanced down at my phone and saw the text from my boyfriend. "I'm here. I'll meet you inside." I didn't want to meet him inside. I didn't want to face the situation. I wanted to be anywhere in the entire universe but where I was. I didn't want to go into that conversation. Although he hadn't spoken the words "I'm breaking up with you," I knew something was off. He'd been distant. I could feel him pulling away. The fact that he wanted to meet up immediately and urgently just confirmed my suspicions. I knew that my best friend and first-ever boyfriend was on the verge of telling me it was over.

I tried to compose myself before walking through that door. Yeah, right. Trying to compose myself was like trying to put a cap on an erupting volcano. My mascara was already a mess. I thought to myself, *I'm going to look like a mangled raccoon. Why can't I at least look good so he'll change his mind? Or at least regret breaking up with me.*

The door opened and closed.

There he was. Nothing had been said yet, but I could tell everything was different. He hadn't officially spoken the words, but it was obvious. I could see it in his eyes.

We didn't hug.

We barely smiled.

It was weird and awkward.

What else would a breakup be besides weird and awkward? There truly wasn't much to be said. He kept things short and to the point. Why drag it out? My soon-to-be-ex-boyfriend told me that we were just too different for one another. He didn't see it working out long term. He said all the nice things to make me feel better and then wished me the best.

He walked me to my car and gave me a hug goodbye. I tried to keep my tears from exploding out of my eyes and pouring all over him. As he turned to go, I reached out and handed him the necklace he'd given me for my birthday. I didn't want it. I didn't need it. It signified too much of what I was losing. He took the necklace from me and walked away.

He was gone. We were done.

I sat in my car and sobbed my eyes out. I felt like I'd been stabbed in the gut and the knife was being twisted. It was heart-wrenching. I hated it. I didn't want it. I didn't plan for this. I had built such a deep friendship with him. We'd made a million memories together. How in the world could I move on? How could I truly say goodbye? How could I continue on in life knowing that my boyfriend and I were going our own separate ways?

It took several months for me to come out of the fog.

By month six, my heart started to feel somewhat intact. My tears started to dry up. I felt like maybe there was hope for the future. Maybe I could love again.

And then it struck me.

What if I go through another breakup in the future? What if I meet a wonderful guy and have my heart broken again. No. No. I can't. I won't.

The thought of going through another breakup began to cripple me. If you've ever been through a tough breakup, you probably know this feeling. My heart desperately ached at the thought of ever having to endure that pain again. I cried over the possibility. I honestly wondered if a life of singleness would be better.

This thought spiraled me into a season of intense worry about my future. I struggled on a daily basis to surrender my plans and my future to God. My hands were clenched into tight fists, and I did not want to release control. I was scared. I was worried. I did not want to get hurt again. If being open to God's plans meant that I might have to go through the process of getting to know a guy, building a friendship, falling in love, and breaking it off, I was not interested.

No thanks.

My tender heart had been hung out to dry, and I was too weak to try for love again.

Post-Breakup Worry

During this season, worry became a constant companion, and I was allowing it to stay. Have you ever felt that way? Like worry was a constant, unwanted companion in your life? I so relate. I knew worrying about the future wasn't the answer to my fears, but I didn't want to turn to God. I knew that if I turned to God, He would ask me to surrender and rest in Him. I didn't want to do that. I wanted to be in control. I wanted to make sure my life was free of the emotional pain I'd once experienced. I bet you know the feeling.

During this worry-ridden post-breakup time of my life, I desperately needed a sister to reach out and show me a better way.

I needed help.

I needed hope.

I needed a loving friend to take me to God's Word and show me the ugly truth about worry. And then I needed that friend to walk with me as I worked toward surrendering my burden of worry to God. I'm beyond grateful to say that I did have several friends and family members who loved me enough to speak some truth into my life. They loved me enough to pull me out of my self-inflicted mess of worry. They held me by the hand, opened up God's Word, and showed me a better way.

Below is one of the passages in Scripture that many sisters and friends encouraged me with. And I want to encourage you with it right now too. This passage brings us hope in the midst of hard seasons. It opens our eyes to see God for who He truly is. It reminds us that we're not alone. God is right beside us. He loves us. He cares for us. And He is with us every step of the way.

> Therefore I tell you, do not be anxious about your life, what you will eat or what you will drink, nor about your body, what you will put on. Is not life more than food, and the body more than clothing? Look at the birds of the air: they

neither sow nor reap nor gather into barns, and yet your heavenly Father feeds them. Are you not of more value than they? And which of you by being anxious can add a single hour to his span of life? And why are you anxious about clothing? Consider the lilies of the field, how they grow: they neither toil nor spin, yet I tell you, even Solomon in all his glory was not arrayed like one of these. But if God so clothes the grass of the field, which today is alive and tomorrow is thrown into the oven, will he not much more clothe you, O you of little faith? Therefore do not be anxious, saying, "What shall we eat?" or "What shall we drink?" or "What shall we wear?" For the Gentiles seek after all these things, and your heavenly Father knows that you need them all. But seek first the kingdom of God and his righteousness, and all these things will be added to you.

Therefore do not be anxious about tomorrow, for tomorrow will be anxious for itself. Sufficient for the day is its own trouble. (Matt. 6:25–34)

This incredibly hope-filled passage is filled with examples of God's great care and love for His creatures. Not just humans but all of His creation. From the littlest of birds to the simplest of flowers. God sees. God cares.

I don't know what you're currently walking through, but maybe this passage in Matthew is exactly what your heart needs right now. Maybe you need the reminder that God sees your pain. He sees your struggles. He cares for you. You are not alone.

From the littlest of birds to the simplest of flowers. God sees. God cares.

If you're wrestling with crippling worry like I was, here's a simple truth that helped me release the weight that was stealing my joy, a truth that will enable each of us to walk in freedom and no longer dread the what-ifs of our future: giving up your worry doesn't mean that you don't care about the problem; it means you take your problem to God and trust Him with the outcome.

Choosing not to worry doesn't mean that you no longer care; it just means that you care deeply enough to need Someone greater to help you carry the burden. It means that you're trusting the only One who can truly comfort your heart and bring you peace. Here is a prayer I prayed that helped me surrender my fears to God and trust Him with my future. I invite you to make it your prayer as well.

> *God, I trust that You will care for me better than I could ever care for myself. I believe that You are the essence of love and will love me better than anyone ever could. Even if I have to go through something difficult again in the future, I know that You will carry me. I know that You will give me peace that surpasses all understanding. You say that You care for the birds of the air and the lilies of the field. If You care for them, I know that You care about me too. Help me to remember that. Help me to trust You. I surrender my burden of worry. I rest in You, Jesus! Amen.*

Choosing to entrust your problems to God will bring a new wave of freedom into your life. You don't have to live shackled to the weight of worry. You are free to enjoy today while trusting God with tomorrow. Instead of dreading your future, you can choose to trust that God will give you the grace you need to handle whatever twists and turns come your way. You can choose to believe that God has always been and will always be faithful. He will never leave you or forsake you.

Whether you're facing a hard breakup like I did or something else, God is able to take you from a place of crippling worry to a place of peaceful rest in Him.

Road Map for Battling Worry

Several years ago, Kristen and I attended a conference where the speakers weren't too concerned about offending anyone with hard-to-hear biblical truth. Don't you just love and hate those speakers? When the two of us received the program with the list of session choices, our eyes were immediately drawn to the session on worry. We were excited to get some biblical encouragement in this area of our lives.

The speaker started out by sharing his thoughts on modern Christians and their relationship to worry. He said that worry has become an "acceptable sin." You know, the sins that we, as Christians, tend to view as not being that big of a deal. Things like speeding (*It's just a little bit faster than the posted speed limit. What's the big deal?*) or gossiping (*Is it really gossip if everyone's talking about it?*) or telling little white lies (*It's not like I'm hurting anyone.*) or cursing (*Everyone does it.*) or worrying (*Who's going to carry the burden of my future if I don't?*).

You get the idea.

We all have our own version of what a big, bad sin is, and then we have our idea of what a small, harmless sin is. The speaker challenged us to figure out which category we put worry in. If we're honest, many of us put worry in the small-sin category. The two of us sure have. Instead of acknowledging how enslaving, heavy, stressful, and burdensome worry is, we just continue on, day after day, and live with it. Many of us have carried the weight of worry for so long that we often forget it's even there.

That conference left the two of us feeling convicted and encouraged. Convicted over the fact that we often dismiss worry as being not that big of a deal and encouraged over the fact that peace is possible.

Worry isn't something that any one of us should take lightly. It's not something any one of us should dismiss as an acceptable sin. God wants so much more for us than worry. He loves us so much that He sent His only Son, Jesus, to die on a cross and rise from the dead to pay the punishment for our sins (John 3:16–18; Rom. 3:23; Rom. 6:23; 1 Cor. 15:3–4). On top of making a way for us to spend eternity with Him in heaven, God also lovingly gave us very clear guidance on how to deal with the sin of worry in our lives. Philippians 4:6–9 says,

> Do not be anxious about anything, but in everything by prayer and supplication with thanksgiving let your requests be made known to God. And the peace of God, which surpasses all understanding, will guard your hearts and your minds in Christ Jesus.
>
> Finally, brothers, whatever is true, whatever is honorable, whatever is just, whatever is pure, whatever is lovely, whatever is commendable, if there is any excellence, if there is anything worthy of praise, think about these things. What you have learned and received and heard and seen in me— practice these things, and the God of peace will be with you.

This passage is one of the clearest road maps for battling worry. God lays out detailed instructions and even promises us peace (not once but twice) as a result of following His loving instructions. This little section in the book of Philippians is our answer to defeating worry. Let's break it down step-by-step to better understand exactly what God is instructing us to do.

1. Do not be anxious (i.e., worry) about anything.
2. Pray about everything.
3. Ask God for your needs.
4. Have a heart of thanksgiving.
5. Take your wants to God.
6. Trust that God's perfect peace will guard your heart.
7. Intentionally guide your thoughts.
8. Only think about things that are true, honorable, just, pure, lovely, commendable, excellent, or worthy of praise.
9. Put all of these steps into practice (by the power of the Holy Spirit inside of you).
10. Trust that the God of peace will be with you.

God wants you to turn to Him with your concerns for today and your fears about tomorrow. He wants to hear from you. He wants to spend time with you through His Word and prayer. This passage shows us that taking our needs to God through prayer is a huge part of battling worry.

It also tells us to intentionally guide our thoughts rather than allowing our thoughts to fuel our emotions in an un-biblical way. We are instructed to intentionally think about

> What's true
> is that God is
> *sovereign,*
> almighty,
> all-powerful,
> and all-loving.

things that are listed in the passage. *Whatever things are true.* What's true? Worrying about things in the future that may never come to pass (like going through another painful breakup) is not necessarily true. What's true is that God is sovereign, almighty, all-powerful, and all-loving.

Choosing to focus on His good character will calm your heart and mind rather than filling it with fear about the unknown.

The list continues on. Read each of the following lines slowly and ask yourself how your thoughts would change if you filtered them through this grid.

Think about whatever is honorable.
Think about whatever is just.
Think about whatever is pure.
Think about whatever is lovely.
Think about whatever is commendable.

If there is any excellence, if there is anything worthy of praise, think about these things.

In the years that followed my breakup, I had opportunity after opportunity to put Philippians 4 into practice. My worst nightmare (going through another breakup) actually became a reality. Not once. Not twice. But three more times. If I'd known during my first breakup that I'd go through three more, I probably would have become a nun. Or a hermit.

I'm so grateful God didn't let me hide in a convent or on top of a mountain though. Throughout each of these trials, God helped me to surrender my fears and trust Him with the future.

He wants to do the same for you.

His faithfulness is constant. His character never changes. You can count on Him. Use Philippians 4 to intentionally guide your thoughts with God's truth. As you do this, the God of peace promises to be with you.

Ponder IT

Choosing not to worry doesn't mean that you don't care about the problem; it means you take your problem to God and trust Him with the outcome.

Remember

✶ God cares for the birds of the air and the lilies and the grass, so how much more does He care for you?

✶ Don't be anxious about tomorrow, for tomorrow will be anxious for itself.

✶ Believe that God has always been and will always be faithful.

✶ Philippians 4:6-9 is your road map for battling worry.

✶ God is the only one who can carry the weight of your worries and give you peace instead.

SHARE YOUR HEART

Dear Lord,

I admit that I am so prone to worry. I worry about little things, and I worry about big things. I acknowledge that worrying is a sin. Worry is carrying a burden that You never asked me to carry. It's exhausting. Please help me to take my cares to You instead. Help me to spend more time in prayer with You. Help me to express my needs to You. Change me from the inside out. I surrender my fears to You and ask You to fill me with Your peace instead. Thank You for loving me and taking care of me. I love You!

Amen.

Consider

—————— **Psalm 23** ——————

The LORD is my shepherd; I shall not want.
　　He makes me lie down in green pastures.
He leads me beside still waters.
　　He restores my soul.
He leads me in paths of righteousness
　　for his name's sake.

Even though I walk through the valley of the shadow of death,
　　I will fear no evil,
for you are with me;
　　your rod and your staff,
　　they comfort me.

You prepare a table before me
    in the presence of my enemies;
you anoint my head with oil;
    my cup overflows.
Surely goodness and mercy shall follow me
    all the days of my life,
and I shall dwell in the house of the LORD
    forever.

Psalm 55:22   Colossians 3:15

Psalm 56:3   1 Peter 5:6-8

Matthew 11:28-30

WHAT **ABOUT YOU?**

1. What causes you to stay up at night and worry?

2. How would you best describe worry?

3. Open your Bible and read Matthew 6:25–34. Underline the words and phrases that stand out most to you. Which of those words or phrases brings you the most hope?

4. How does worrying about tomorrow steal today's joy?

5. What needs to change in your life in order for you to open up your clenched fists and trust God with your worries?

Go
FOR IT   Pull out a timer and set it for three minutes. Now use those three minutes to meditate on Philippians 4:6-7. Basically, read this passage over and over, and ponder what it means.

Do not be anxious about anything, but in everything by prayer and supplication with thanksgiving let your requests be made known to God. And the peace of God, which surpasses all understanding, will guard your hearts and your minds in Christ Jesus.

After you've meditated, ask yourself this question: What needs to change in my life in order to obey God's instructions in this passage?

Look at the *birds* of the air:
they neither sow nor reap
nor gather into barns,
and yet your heavenly
Father *feeds* them.
Are you not of more
value than they?

Matthew 6:26

chapter 4

The Bright Side
of Disappointment

It had been over five years since I (Bethany) hung up that sparkling white wedding dress in the back of my closet. My starry-eyed dreams of floating down the aisle to my handsome prince were nowhere in sight.

Do you want to know what was in sight though? Dust bunnies. Lots and lots of dust bunnies just making my dress their home.

Sometimes I'd catch sight of that wedding dress, and it would feel like a fresh punch to the gut. My mind would instantly fill with negative thoughts. *You're not married. You'll never get married. You'll probably end up an old maid, rocking her life away, knitting on the front porch.* Per the usual, I'd quickly push the clothes back in place and try to cover the wedding dress. I didn't want to be reminded of how differently my life was turning out from what I'd expected. I didn't want to be reminded of how stupid I felt for spending over a thousand dollars on that unworn dress. I didn't want the fresh reminder of how lonely I was.

I'll never forget the afternoon my little wedding-dress secret almost got out. I was doing some painting in my bedroom, and a few friends were helping me out. We moved the furniture to the middle of the room and got to work. We chatted, listened to music, ate pizza, and had a great time. Until one of my friends tried to look in my closet. I saw her open the closet doors and reach toward *that* side of the closet. The forbidden side. The side with my hush-hush secret.

I couldn't let my secret out. Not yet.

I was too embarrassed. Too ashamed. Too not in the mood to explain.

Without even thinking, I sprinted across the room and slammed the closet doors shut. "You can't look in there," I told her. "There's . . . um . . . some secret gifts . . . and . . . um . . . I don't want anyone to see them . . . ha-ha."

It was awkward. She knew I wasn't totally telling the truth, but she didn't press. She let it go, and that was that. We finished painting, and everyone went home.

That night I found myself lying in bed with my single status blaring in my face. I wondered what it would be like to actually walk down the aisle wearing my dress. And even more, what would it be like to have a husband to do life with? My eyes wandered toward my closet doors, and I wondered if that would ever become my reality.

Disappointment filled my heart, and tears filled my eyes. In the dark silence of my upstairs bedroom, I let the tears fall.

Disappointment Knocks on Everyone's Door

Life is filled with moments, hours, days, and years that are anything but what we'd hoped they'd be. Disappointment is a reality we all must face. Sometimes it's a crushing weight that feels all-consuming (e.g., losing a loved one unexpectedly), and sometimes it's just a little desire that goes unfulfilled (e.g., driving to your favorite coffee shop only to realize that it's closed). Whatever the case for you personally, disappointments are a regular part of life.

What disappointments have you already faced, just in this past week? Day? Hour?

If we don't learn how to handle our disappointments (big or small) in a biblical way, they will leave us crushed, hopeless, or just feeling like we got the raw end of the deal.

Throughout the Bible, we see a lot of examples of regular people who faced serious disappointment.

We see Esther's life story of major ups and downs in the Old Testament, the book of Esther. Although God used her to help save His people (the Jews) from being eliminated, she experienced much disappointment in her life. She was an orphan raised by her cousin, Mordecai. She was then ripped from her cousin's home and forced to enter a beauty competition to become queen. If she won, she would marry one of the most powerful and evil men on earth. If she lost, she would lead a lonely life as a concubine to this king. She won, and the hardship had only begun. She had to put her life on the line to save the very people she'd been taken from. God used her for "such a time as this" (Esther 4:14), but her life truly was the opposite of what she ever would have planned.

67

In Genesis 37–50, we see that Joseph's story is riddled with difficulty as well. He faced disappointment after disappointment. None of which was even a result of his own doing. He was a victim at the hands of his own brothers' abusive treatment. He was sold into slavery by his brothers, falsely accused of committing a crime, and thrown into a dungeon for many years. But despite all that was stacked against him, he chose to honor God and forgive those who had hurt him. After all this, he said something extraordinary to his brothers: "As for you, you meant evil against me, but God meant it for good" (Gen. 50:20).

Fast-forward a few thousand years, and we see that disappointment is a regular occurrence for modern-day women just like you and the two of us.

Disappointment comes in all shapes and sizes.

Take our friend Anna, for example. She met the man of her dreams (or so she thought) and was headed toward her happily ever after. It took only two years for her marriage to come crashing down. Her husband left her for another woman. Nothing she said or did would make him stay. He'd found his new "soul mate" and was moving on. Anna was crushed. Talk about a devastating disappointment.

Then there's our friend Lana. She'd picked up her life and moved across the country for her dream job. It was everything she'd ever hoped for out of a career and more. Her dreams came crashing down two months after she moved. The company she'd gone to work for was bought out and her position was eliminated. She found herself jobless and in a new city with hardly any friends. What a disappointment.

And there's our friend Shawna. She'd always dreamed of growing up and having tight-knit relationships with her siblings and parents. Family was a big deal to her, and she wanted her family to be close. Unfortunately, that didn't become a part of her story. Due to bitterness and unforgiveness between her parents, Shawna's family was divided. Her mom and dad were forcing Shawna and her siblings to take sides. This tore her family apart. Shawna experienced disappointment in the one way she hoped she'd never have to.

Little disappointments, large disappointments, and life-altering disappointments happen to everyone. It doesn't matter who you are, where you were born, how much money you have, or how popular you are, disappointment knocks on everyone's door at some point or another.

Finding Joy in the Midst of Disappointment

The question we should be asking isn't "Will I experience disappointment?" but rather "How can I still find joy in the midst of my disappointment when it strikes?" Over the past few years, God has been teaching the two of us a lot about finding joy in the midst of our own disappointments. As we've walked through hardships, like infertility, miscarriage, singleness, an unworn wedding dress, the death of our baby

> True joy and real suffering can *coexist.*

brother, the deaths of grandparents, the sudden passing of a good friend, a sports injury that put one of us on the basketball bench in high school for months at a time, the unexpected loss of a pet, and a broken friendship, God has shown us that it's possible to have joy despite our circumstances.

We've come to understand that true joy and real suffering can coexist.

We're not perfect at this. We often find ourselves wrestling with God's Word and asking Him to change our circumstances. But, at the end of the day, we know that disappointment doesn't have to steal our joy.

We love how one author offers her perspective on this topic.

> God promises that those who seek him lack no good thing (Psalm 34:10). In reality, our most painful disappointments often seem like God's withholding of a good thing from us. . . . But if God is always working for the good of those who love him (Romans 8:28), then either what we longed for—in the exact way and at the precise time we desired it—was not good, or else God is not finished redeeming this disappointment for good. And in the meantime, we have God himself. He alone is good (Matthew 19:17). Every good and perfect gift comes from him (James 1:17). With him as our shepherd, goodness will follow us all the days of our lives (Psalm 23:6). And nothing—not even the most devastating disappointment—can separate us from his love (Romans 8:31–39). Every disappointment I've faced has been a humbling and convicting invitation to test whether my heart truly seeks after one thing—to dwell with, gaze upon, and inquire of God alone (Psalm 27:4). God is the ultimate and only all-satisfying good. No disappointments can take him from us, but they can often point us to him.[1]

Instead of allowing our lives to become disillusioned by our disappointment, let's choose to press into God in the midst of the struggle. *Okay,* you might be thinking, *that sounds great and spiritual and like the right thing to do . . . but how exactly do we do that? How do we draw near to God in the midst of our unfulfilled longings?*

The two of us want to share with you four practical ways that God has helped us to press into our relationship with Him and find joy in the midst of our own disappointments. We hope these truths will equip you to find true joy in the midst of yours as well.

1. Humbly submit to God's story for your life.

Discontentment and friction often arise in our hearts when we forget who holds the pen to our story. When we look around and begin comparing our story to those of others, we lose sight of the fact that God has every person on a different path. His timing is not the same for all of us. His plan is tailor-made for our individual journey and for our greater good.

I (Bethany) wrestled with this as I found myself injured and on the bench for varsity basketball during my senior year of high school. Basketball was my life at the time, and this injury was devastating for me. No more final home games. No more senior moments. I was done. I watched my friends enjoy their senior year, injury-free, and graduate happily ever after. Although this was very difficult for me, God gently worked on my heart and reminded me through His Word that my life story was His to write. My life story was different than my teammates', and God had a good plan for me.

Even though I wished I could have finished my senior year on a high note, I was reminded of truths from His Word, like "Why are you cast down, O my soul, and why are you in turmoil within me? Hope in God; for I shall again praise him, my salvation and my God" (Ps. 42:11), and "Your kingdom come, your will be done, on earth as it is in heaven" (Matt. 6:10).

Humbly submitting my life to God's story for me was my first step toward true joy, and it's your first step as well.

2. Trust that God's plan is for your good.

We live in a time where *good* means getting what you want. The good life is focused on personal happiness and making all of our dreams come true. But God's version of *good* is the opposite of this. (We'll dig deeper into God's goodness in chapter 5.) It isn't surface-level or as flimsy as our mood. God knows that true and lasting satisfaction can only come from becoming more like Christ and by loving God more fully. Our circumstances are not the defining factor of our joy and hope. God's version of *good* might look like allowing challenging circumstances into our lives that serve to remind us of our need for Him.

I (Kristen) have wrestled with this truth repeatedly. Every time I find myself giving in to discouragement over my season of infertility, I remind myself that *good* doesn't mean getting what I want when I want it. I choose to soak my heart in Scripture passages like Psalm 119:68, which says, "You are good and do good; teach me your statutes," and Ephesians 2:10, which reminds us that "we are his workmanship, created in Christ Jesus for good works, which God prepared beforehand, that we should walk in them."

Trusting that God's plan is for your good is the second step toward true joy.

3. Serve God wholeheartedly right now.

Many of us struggle with the weight of our disappointments so much that it becomes a barrier that keeps us from moving forward. We begin to view our identity and life through the lens of our unfulfilled longings rather than through our identity as a daughter of God. God wants us to lay our desires at the foot of His altar and offer them as a sacrifice of worship to Him. He wants to use us to build His kingdom in unique ways right now. He doesn't need our circumstances to change in order for us to live for Him wholeheartedly.

Over the past several years, we've each had to reframe our mindset about what it means to be successful or faithful. God hasn't given me (Kristen) a healthy pregnancy yet, and so I've had more time and energy to pour into the lives of young women in my community and through Girl Defined. Rather than dwelling on what I didn't have (children), I strove to be faithful with what I did have (discipleship opportunities).

God didn't give me (Bethany) a husband until I was thirty. I learned to use that time to pour into my church, encourage other single ladies, invest into my family, and live all out for Christ right where He had me. I learned how to truly thrive in that season. I even had the opportunity to cowrite a book with Kristen on the topic (*Love Defined: Embracing God's Vision for Lasting Love and Satisfying Relationships*) and encourage other girls who were walking through a similar season.

Regardless of your season of life, Matthew 6:20–21 can be an anchor for your heart just like it was (and is) for ours. "But lay up for yourselves treasures in heaven, where neither moth nor rust destroys and where thieves do not break in and steal. For where your treasure is, there your heart will be also."

Serving God wholeheartedly right now is the third step toward true joy.

4. Keep your eyes focused on your future hope.

Disappointments, as hard as they are, give us an opportunity to cling to Jesus like He is all we have. In a weird sort of way, they become the very means to push us closer to what our soul needs most: more of Jesus. With that perspective, our disappointments become meaningful and purpose-filled seasons in our lives. They also remind us on a regular basis that we need Jesus because we live in a broken world. The pain, disappointments, loss, and brokenness we face are a direct result of the fallen world we live in. They are a temporary reality.

Because of Christ's death on the cross and His resurrection, we can look through our earthly disappointments to a future hope and joy that will last for all eternity. As one writer reminds us, "There is a day, an eternal day in the not-too-distant future, when all disappointment will be taken away and when all things will not only be new but will remain new. Every possible source of disappointment will be removed, and all our hopes will be fulfilled."[2]

> Because of Christ's death on the cross and His *resurrection*, we can look through our earthly disappointments to a future hope and joy that will last for all *eternity*.

Having this future hope has been a huge encouragement for me (Bethany). When I found myself staring at that wedding dress over and over again, I desperately needed hope. I needed to know that the heartache, tears, and unfulfilled longings wouldn't last forever. I needed to remind myself of truths like "Let us hold fast the confession of our hope without wavering, for he who promised is faithful" (Heb. 10:23), and "But they who wait for the LORD shall renew their strength; they shall mount up with wings like eagles; they shall run and not be weary; they shall walk and not faint" (Isa. 40:31).

Keeping your eyes on your future hope in Jesus is your fourth step toward true joy.

The next time you find yourself struggling with a disappointment, remind yourself of the four steps toward true joy:

1. Humbly submit to God's story for your life.
2. Trust that God's plan is for your good.
3. Serve God wholeheartedly right now.
4. Keep your eyes focused on your future hope.

He Holds the Future

Even as my wedding dress continued to hang in the back of my closet for many more years, I learned to have hope in the promises from God's Word. Memorizing the different passages I shared with you in this chapter was a huge part of my journey from disappointment to true joy. Having the ability to fill my mind with truth was priceless.

The two of us really encourage you to memorize at least two or three of the Bible verses we shared throughout this chapter. Hiding God's Word in your heart will enable you to recall truth in the moments you most need it.

Always remember that your hope is in Christ, and your future is with Him. True and lasting joy can be had. When disappointment strikes, cling to the hope that is found in your relationship with Jesus. Cling to your Savior, knowing that He will sustain you through every hard moment. Because in Him, there is hope for the good days, the bad days, and every day in between.

Ponder IT

> **True joy and real suffering can coexist.**

Remember

★ We will all face disappointment in this life.

★ The thing you must trust God for most right now is the very thing He wants to use to draw you closer to Him.

★ Cling to your Savior, knowing that He will sustain you through every hard moment.

★ Disappointments, as hard as they are, give us an opportunity to cling to Jesus like He is all we have.

★ Because of Christ's death on the cross and His resurrection, we can look through our earthly disappointments to a future hope and joy that will last for all eternity.

SHARE YOUR HEART

Dear Lord,

I just want to say it out loud: life is hard. It's hard to experience disappointment. I don't like it. Please help me to find hope in the fact that this life isn't my eternity. One day I will spend forever with You. Thank You for that hope. Thank You for Jesus. Help me to run to You when I face disappointment. Use the hard moments in my life to deepen my relationship with You. Thank You for reminding me that my disappointments aren't meaningless.

Amen.

Consider

Isaiah 40:28–31

Have you not known? Have you not heard?
The LORD is the everlasting God,
    the Creator of the ends of the earth.
He does not faint or grow weary;
    his understanding is unsearchable.
He gives power to the faint,
    and to him who has no might he increases strength.
Even youths shall faint and be weary,
    and young men shall fall exhausted;
but they who wait for the LORD shall renew their strength;
    they shall mount up with wings like eagles;
they shall run and not be weary;
    they shall walk and not faint.

---

1 Peter 5:10-11

And after you have suffered a little while, the God of all grace, who has called you to his eternal glory in Christ, will himself restore, confirm, strengthen, and establish you. To him be the dominion forever and ever. Amen.

DEEPER

Psalm 16:11   Psalm 104

Psalm 42:11   Psalm 119:68

Psalm 103:1

WHAT **ABOUT** YOU?

1. What is your greatest disappointment at this moment in your life?

2. How is it possible to have true joy in the midst of real suffering?

3. In what ways have you doubted God's goodness due to your disappointment?

4. How does Psalm 34:10 bring you hope?

5. Open up your Bible to the last book and read Revelation 21:1-5. God is preparing an eternal home where He will dwell with you face-to-face. How does that promise encourage you to press on?

6. What would it look like if you truly clung to Jesus in the midst of disappointment?

Go
FOR IT   Open up your Bible and read through the story of Joseph in Genesis 37–50. His life was filled with great disappointment. What would change in your life if you responded to disappointment like Joseph did? If you trusted God so much that you could say, "As for you, you meant evil against me, but God meant it for good"?

Journal your thoughts and share what your life would look like if you responded to disappointment like Joseph did.

You make known
to me the path of life;
in your presence
there is fullness of *joy*;
at your right hand
are *pleasures*
forevermore.

Psalm 16:11

chapter 5

God, Are You Even Good?

My (Kristen's) second miscarriage happened two weeks after my twenty-seventh birthday. What started off as an amazing, hope-filled new year took an unexpected turn for the worse. Since my birthday is on January 7, the festivities and excitement from Christmas and New Year's always linger on.

But not this year.

This year was supposed to be *my* year. The year that everything turned right. The year my sorrows from the first miscarriage (six months earlier) would be overshadowed by the joy of this new pregnancy. But instead, it felt like the Grinch had ripped away everything beautiful and happy. The sound of Christmas carols and New Year's fireworks suddenly grated on my heart as a wave of grief washed over me.

How could this be happening to me again?! I questioned as a stream of tears blurred my vision. I had researched the statistics of recurring miscarriages online, and the numbers were low. Most women who experience one miscarriage go on to have healthy pregnancies.

But not me.

When the cramping and bleeding started at around six and a half weeks, Zack immediately drove me to the hospital. After a quick and very uncomfortable ultrasound, my doctor told me that everything looked fine. She even played the sound of the baby's heartbeat through the speakers for us to hear. As I watched that tiny pulsing flicker on the screen, a spark of hope flickered inside my own heart.

"I'm not sure what's causing the bleeding," my doctor said, "but the heartbeat is strong and your uterus looks good."

As Zack drove me back home, we didn't say much. He simply held my hand with a firm and loving grip, reminding me that I wasn't alone. Several hours later, things took a turn for the worse. We texted my doctor to tell her exactly what was happening. Her words were brief, compassionate, and honest.

"Kristen, I'm so sorry to say this, but it sounds like you're having a miscarriage. Please don't hesitate to take pain meds as needed. Again, I am so sorry. I'm here if you need anything."

By 10:00 p.m. the miscarriage had happened.

"I don't understand . . . everything was fine . . . I can't bear this again!" I told Zack in anguish as he held me close. We cried together all night.

The next few weeks and months were extremely hard as I walked the same path of grief again. Not only were my dreams of motherhood eluding me, but they were also warping into the same nightmare again. As my three-year wedding anniversary approached the following summer, my empty arms felt heavy. Why would God allow this to happen to me twice? Why didn't He stop this second miscarriage? Why would He take my baby away again? Doesn't He see the pain I'm enduring?

I had far more questions than answers.

During this hard season, Bethany and I were chatting one day about how challenging and unpredictable life can be. We both acknowledged that our lives weren't really turning out the way we had expected. I was grieving the loss of a second pregnancy, and she was trudging through the valley of an intensely hard breakup. Just when we both thought we were taking a step forward in the game of life, we found ourselves back at square one. No baby for me. No marriage for her.

What was God doing? What was the point of all this? We both wrestled with the same question: *If God is good, why would He allow this?* Theologically, we knew that God was good because the Bible said so, but we needed more than that. We needed to know *how* He was still good in the midst of so much pain and loss. Why was He allowing these trials into our lives?

I know we're not alone in asking these questions. This is probably one of the most common questions that Christians wrestle with: *Why would a good God allow such hard things to happen to people?* Have you wrestled with that? As Christians, we typically ask this question when we're walking through a dark valley. Most of us don't question God's goodness when we're surrounded by daisies and butterflies with a latte in our hand. We question God's character when life becomes pain-filled and hard. When we hit rock bottom.

When our pillow is stained with tears. It's in those moments that we wonder if God loves us. If He sees us. If He even cares about our circumstances.

Thankfully, our Creator isn't surprised by or afraid of our questions. He's not shocked that we're struggling to trust Him. As the Psalms remind us, "He is mindful that we are nothing but dust" (Ps. 103:14 NASB). He knows we're frail humans. And He wants to help us bring our struggles to Him so that we can work through them together. He wants to comfort our broken hearts through the ointment of His Word. As Matthew 11:28 gently reminds us,

> Come to me, all who labor and are heavy laden, and I will give you rest.

Let's come to Him right now. Together. As sisters. Let's each bring our pain, struggles, brokenness, and questions to God's Word to see what He says. Let's work through this thing together. If God truly is *good*, let's find out.

Does God Care about My Suffering?

Remember that time when there was a worldwide toilet paper shortage and everyone rushed to the stores to buy it? Full disclosure here. I was one of those people. I know, I know. I wouldn't have gone except for the fact that I was completely out of toilet paper. Like legitimately. I've never waited in a line that long to buy toilet paper in my life. It was unbelievable. Not only that, but people were stressed and mad. Nobody was smiling. The tension was real. I eventually got my pack of toilet paper and went on my way. Thankfully, the TP shortage didn't last forever, and the shelves were restocked with fluffy white rolls of goodness. Who knew shopping for TP could be so eventful!

The TP shortage sparked a sea of funny memes and GIFs on social media, but it also revealed something deeper about us as humans. We don't handle the *unexpected* very well. Even when it involves toilet paper. When life throws us a curveball, we're quick to get mad. We're quick to be rude. Am I right? Deep in our hearts we're prone to believe that the good life is free from any inconveniences or hardships.

This is the attitude we often carry with us into all of life. From the little things to the big things.

As a result of this mindset, most of us feel totally blindsided when the really hard things strike. We feel shocked. We feel confused. We instantly question God's character and His goodness. We question His love. We think to ourselves, *God, if You truly cared for me, You would change my circumstances. You wouldn't allow this to happen!* And so, in our pain, we judge God's character through the lens of our circumstances. We decide that He must not be a very good God after all. *If He was good, He would give me the good life.*

This is exactly how I (Kristen) felt after my second miscarriage. I remember sitting in my bedroom alone one afternoon, wrestling with all sorts of feelings toward God. To be honest, I was mad at Him. He didn't feel good to me. He didn't feel loving to me. He allowed one of the most precious gifts I had ever been given to be taken away. Surely a loving God wouldn't do that. Surely a loving Father would spare me from so much pain, right?

And that is where I took my first wrong turn.

You've probably taken this wrong turn too.

As modern Christians we often have this idea that our lives should be supernaturally protected from major pain and suffering. We imagine some sort of puffy white heavenly cloud of protection guarding us from all outside danger. Wouldn't that be nice? But the Bible never promises us this. In fact, it promises us the opposite of a puffy white cloud. First Peter 4:12 literally says,

> Beloved, do not be surprised at the fiery trial when it comes upon you to test you, as though something strange were happening to you.

Ouch. The Bible tells us to *expect* trials. The Bible warns us to not be surprised. Apparently, trials are a normal part of human existence. Nobody is off the hook. Even Jesus Himself experienced trials and suffering when He came to this earth. And He was perfect. If anyone deserved a puffy white cloud, it was Him. But what happened to Him? He suffered. A lot.

Think about it.

Unlike all other world religions, the God of the Bible is personally acquainted with grief and pain. He knows what suffering is on an intimate level. We might picture God as a tall, gray-haired old man sitting in heaven looking down for someone to squash. But throughout the Old and New Testaments we see a surprisingly unexpected picture of God. He's not some sort of angry wizard who sits high on His throne, smirking at the pain and suffering of those beneath Him. Not even close.

By His own choice, Jesus left His glorious and perfect home in heaven to enter our dirty and broken world. He took on the body of a human so that He could walk with us, talk with us, cry with us, speak to us, and save us. *He came to us.* He entered our mess. He faced the pain of this world, though He deserved none of it. He was rejected by humans, mocked, beaten, stripped of His dignity, and ultimately nailed to a wooden cross. He willingly chose a life of suffering in order to give us new life. He died to pay the penalty for sin that we deserved (John 3:16).

He willingly chose a life of suffering in order to give us new life.

That—right there—is the character of our Savior.

He's not a distant God who's detached from human experiences and pain but an intimate, relational, and loving Father who walks with His children through their suffering.

If you're struggling to believe that God loves you because of your hard circumstances, allow this beautiful gospel reality to recapture your heart right now: *You, my sister, are so loved by Jesus, that He willingly left His perfect place in heaven to live a human life filled with suffering, pain, rejection, and loss—and He did this for the ultimate purpose of redeeming humanity by dying a painful death on a cross so that you could be saved. That's how much He loves you.*

The gospel shows us how incredible God's love is for us. Only a loving and sacrificial God would die to save His people. That is our God. We need to remind our hearts of the cross, over and over again.

The next time you're sitting in that moment of intense pain because someone you love rejected you, remember that Jesus understands because He was rejected too. The next time you're struck with the awful memories of abuse that happened to you, remember that Jesus understands because

He endured physical harm and abuse at the hands of others too. (Please see p. 110 regarding abuse.) The next time you're crushed under the weight of grief, remember that Jesus understands because He grieved too. The next time you find yourself sitting alone, with tears streaming down your face, turn to God and say, *God, I feel so much pain right now. Please help me.* Then take a moment to pause and remember the cross. Remind your pain-filled heart of the deep love that your Father has for you as His daughter. He understands your suffering because He's suffered too. He loves you, and is with you in this moment of grief. You are not alone.

When you view your pain and suffering through the lens of the cross, you'll see a loving God who cares for you. A God who is opposed to sin and evil. A God who loves you deeply and who fully understands the pain you're walking through. Suffering becomes bearable when we know God is with us.

Changed by God's Unchanging Character

Learning to view God's character through the lens of the cross was so helpful for me (Kristen) during the aftermath of my second miscarriage. My feelings told me that God was far away and didn't care about me. But God's Word told me something different. As I sat on my couch one morning with my Bible in hand, I realized that I had been listening to my feelings about God rather than listening to His Word. I was letting my emotions tell me how to view God's character instead of letting His Word inform my perspective.

I knew I needed a good dose of truth.

So, I brewed a delicious cup of hot coffee (this is an essential step; let's be real, coffee makes everything a little better), and I opened up my Bible. Instead of just reading a random passage of Scripture, I started looking up specific verses that talked about the character of God. As my coffee perked up my energy, God's Word began perking up my soul. Instead of trying to convince myself that God is good, I allowed the Bible to show me why He is good.

Character quality after character quality revealed God's true nature.

I set my coffee down and began to cry a little.

God's character was so beautiful and perfect and loving . . . I had just been too blinded by my anger to see it. I grabbed a piece of paper and started writing down every character quality I could find. I even did a quick internet search to figure out where I could find more in the Bible.

Here are some of the ones I discovered:

God Is Wise (Rom. 11:33)

God Is Faithful (Deut. 7:9)

God Is Good (Ps. 34:8)

God Is All-Powerful (Ps. 33:6)

God Is Just (Deut. 32:4)

God Is Infinite (Col. 1:17)

God Is Merciful (Rom. 9:15–16)

God Is All-Knowing (Isa. 46:9–10)

God Is Gracious (Ps. 145:8)

God Is Immutable (Mal. 3:6)

God Is Loving (1 John 4:7–8)

God Is Holy (Rev. 4:8)

God Is Glorious (Hab. 3:4)

And this is only scratching the surface.

With each new attribute I discovered, my hard heart was softened by God's incredible character. I needed more of this. So I decided to divide these character qualities into thirty days and study one per day. I guess you could call it a thirty-day devotional on the character of God.

Y'all, it was powerful.

Each morning I would spend a few minutes meditating on one character quality, then I would study the specific passage of Scripture that talked about it. Finally, I would close in prayer, thanking God for His character. After thirty days of this, my heart was soaring. No coffee needed! My spirit felt revived by simply remembering who God is.

> God is *good*, even when we don't feel like He is.

If you're struggling to believe that God is good, I can't encourage you enough to do this thirty-day study. Just grab a journal and use my list to get started. To discover even more attributes of God's character, check out the 30-day resource we created over at www.GirlDefined.com/God.

God is good, even when we don't feel like He is. When we view our trials through the lens of His character and the cross, we will see an amazing God who loves us and understands our suffering.

The Tears Won't Last Forever

My (Kristen's) miscarriages were painfully hard on every level. I still don't know why they happened. God hasn't given me a direct answer. He probably never will. But I do know this: God has used those hard valleys to deepen my relationship with Him in profound ways. As I watched my dream of becoming a mom fade into grief, God comforted me and held me close. Instead of believing the lies that I was barren, useless, and a failure—I looked to Christ for my identity and found fruitfulness, purpose, and life in Him. God has also opened so many doors for me to share my story with other women who are walking through similar losses. I've been able to encourage women in unique ways as a result of what I've walked through.

Looking back now, I can see that my suffering and loss have not been in vain. Your suffering and loss do not have to be in vain either. As heavy as the burden may feel today, the weight won't last forever. The story isn't over yet. Right now, we're living during a time that some people call "between two gardens." We are beyond the perfect garden of Eden in Genesis, but we haven't arrived yet to the day when God makes all things new *again* (Rev. 21:5).

Jesus came once, and He's coming back again.

The final part of God's plan is to restore our broken world back to paradise and to restore our face-to-face relationship with Him. Revelation 21:4 tells us, "He will wipe away every tear from their eyes, and death shall be no more, neither shall there be mourning, nor crying, nor pain anymore, for the former things have passed away." What a glorious day that will be.

That's what we have to look forward to.

But we're not there yet. And in the meantime, God isn't done working in our lives. He sees our current suffering and pain, and He cares deeply about us. Our suffering isn't meaningless to Him: "We know that for those who love God all things work together for good, for those who are called according to his purpose" (Rom. 8:28). What a promise. God wants to use our stories of brokenness to tell the bigger story of His plan of redemption. As He redeems our lives from the pit and sets our feet on solid ground, our scars tell the story of a Savior who rescues His people. As we press on through the storms and cling to Christ for our strength, our lives become beacons of hope to the sisters around us. Our trials only make us stronger. As Romans 5:3–5 says,

> Not only that, but we rejoice in our sufferings, knowing that suffering produces endurance, and endurance produces character, and character produces hope, and hope does not put us to shame, because God's love has been poured into our hearts through the Holy Spirit who has been given to us.

I'll never forget the first time I spoke about my miscarriages from the stage at a Girl Defined Conference. I got so choked up, I couldn't even finish my sentence. I just stood there in silence, staring out at hundreds of big watching eyes. Bethany graciously stepped in to talk for me. That was hard. Even awkward. But as a result of opening up, I had dozens of young women come up to me afterward and share their own stories of loss and pain. We were able to connect with one another in a deep way and encourage each other to press on.

God produced beauty out of the ashes of my loss.

He was showing me, one day at a time, that He is good. His character is constant. He never changes. He is always the same. I can joyfully join the psalmist in saying, "Oh give thanks to the LORD, for he is good" (Ps. 107:1).

Friend, no matter what you're walking through right now, God cares for you, and He is good. *Take your burden to the cross.* Pour out your heart to your loving and good Father, and ask Him to strengthen you for the journey ahead. God loves you and is working in your life. Right now. Just like He did for me, He wants to produce beauty from your ashes.

We're all tempted to question God's goodness and character in the midst of trials and losses, but when we view our circumstances through the lens of the gospel, we find mercy, grace, and hope. We can have full confidence and assurance that God is good, because He *is*. Oh, so very good.

Ponder IT

> God isn't some sort of distant deity who's detached from human experiences and pain but an intimate, relational, and loving Father who walks with His children through their suffering.

Remember

✴ God's not afraid of our questions. He's not shocked that we're struggling to trust Him.

✴ He wants to help us bring our deepest struggles to Him so that we can work through them together.

✴ Rather than viewing God's character through the lens of our circumstances, we need to view our circumstances through the lens of God's character.

✴ No matter what you're walking through right now, God cares for you, and He is good. Take your burden to the cross.

SHARE **YOUR** HEART

Dear Lord,

I confess that I'm tempted to doubt Your character when I'm going through hard times.

Thank You for reminding me of Your amazing grace and love through the cross. I am so comforted by the fact that You understand suffering and can relate to what I'm walking through. You have experienced pain, rejection, and abuse—and You did that for me. Thank You for the hope I have in the gospel! Help me to remember that You are always working behind the scenes of my life. You have a purpose for my suffering that is greater than what I can see. Refine me and make me more like Jesus. You are my good, good Father.

Amen.

Consider

——— **Psalm 34:1-8** ———

I will bless the LORD at all times;
 his praise shall continually be in my mouth.
My soul makes its boast in the LORD;
 let the humble hear and be glad.
Oh, magnify the LORD with me,
 and let us exalt his name together!

I sought the LORD, and he answered me
 and delivered me from all my fears.

Those who look to him are radiant,
   and their faces shall never be ashamed.
This poor man cried, and the Lord heard him
   and saved him out of all his troubles.
The angel of the Lord encamps
   around those who fear him, and delivers them.

Oh, taste and see that the Lord is good!
   Blessed is the man who takes refuge in him!

DIG DEEPER

Psalm 100   James 1:1-15
Romans 8:18-30   Revelation 4:7-11

WHAT **ABOUT YOU?**

1. Looking back on your life, was there a hard valley that caused you to question God's character and goodness? What happened?

2. How does Jesus's earthly life and death bring you comfort and hope in your own suffering?

3. Looking back at the attributes of God, which one do you find most encouraging?

4. When hard times strike, what (or whom) are you tempted to run toward for strength instead of Christ (e.g., a spouse, a friend, food, entertainment, busyness, etc.)?

5. How have you seen God use your trials to strengthen your faith in Him?

Go
FOR IT   Grab your journal or a piece of
paper. Now look back at the attributes of God that we
listed near the end of this chapter. Take some time
to write down each attribute of God, along with a
short prayer of thanks for that specific character quality. Don't rush past this. Meditating on God's faithful
character will bring so much peace and hope to your
heart.

Oh give *thanks* to the Lord, for he is *good.*

Psalm 107:1

chapter 6

Hello, Crazy-Girl Emotions

There once lived two little girls who cried their eyes out over a hamster and a vacuum cleaner. Yes, a hamster and a vacuum cleaner. Welcome to our childhood. We (Kristen and Bethany) cried our eyes out on this particular day. Here's what happened.

This situation took place during our preteen years. It all started when our family purchased a couple of hamsters as pets. The two of us loved these hamsters. We fed them, played with them, cared for them, and tried to give them happy hamster lives. Long story short, our hamsters fell in love and had quite a few babies. Those babies grew up and had some more babies. What started out as two hamsters quickly multiplied into a dozen hamsters.

Things were getting out of control.

After much deliberation and discussion, our parents decided that we were done with the hamster farm. They did their best to find new homes for the sweet little things and sent them on their merry little hamster way.

It wasn't merry for us though. We were heartbroken.

The tears poured out. We sobbed and sobbed and sobbed. Our little preteen selves were quickly losing control of our already fragile emotions. The night continued on, and we found ourselves crying about everything. We mean *everything*. We were emotionally wrecked over our little pets, and things were taking a turn for the worse. After hours of crying in the living room, I (Kristen) turned to Bethany with tear-stained eyes and randomly said, "I feel so bad for the vacuum cleaner. It works so hard and no one appreciates it. They just use it and shove it in a corner. Sometimes people even kick it if it's not working right. The poor vacuum!"

Bethany looked back at me with tears flowing down her cheeks and said, "You're right! No one appreciates the vacuum cleaner! How sad!"

Forget National Geographic. Cue the reality show.

We both spent the next several minutes literally crying over our faithful, old family vacuum cleaner. I'm pretty sure our siblings thought their older sisters had totally lost it. And to be honest, we had. Crying over hamsters is one thing, but crying over a vacuum cleaner is a whole new level of crazy.

Hamsters. Vacuum cleaners. Hormones.

Tears. Drama. Crazy-girl emotions.

And we weren't even teenagers yet.

When Emotions Take Over

We know we're not alone in this. If you dug into your childhood stories right now, I'm sure you could recall some hilarious cry-fests of your own. Let's be real though. We don't need to dig into our childhood to find these stories, do we? Little-girl tears turn into teenage tears. And teenage tears turn into womanhood tears. And if you happen to be one of the rare females who never cries, this doesn't mean you're off the hook. We all have strong emotions and feelings; we just might express them differently (i.e., those who clam up vs. those who blow up, right?).

Emotions come in all shapes and sizes. And they're not a bad thing. God created us to be emotional. Emotions help us to feel deeply about things that matter. To laugh when something's funny. To grieve when we walk through a loss. To connect with people in an intimate way. Emotions are a powerful force. They have the ability to take us to the highest of heights and the lowest of valleys. From the greatest of joys to the deepest of sorrows. They're extremely influential in our lives.

Unfortunately, ever since the fall (read Gen. 3), our emotions have been greatly impacted by sin. Therefore, what we feel isn't always what is right and true. Raise your hand if you've ever made a dumb decision in the midst of hot emotions, then regretted it three seconds later. Yep, go ahead and raise both hands if needed. Guilty too!

This less-beautiful side of our emotions is strong and can easily rule us if we're not careful. That's when our emotions get out of line. That's when we become girls who are driven by our *feelings* rather than by what's true. We begin to view

> God created us to be *emotional*. Emotions help us to feel deeply about things that *matter*.

our circumstances through the lens of our *emotions* rather than God's Word.

When it comes to your emotions and feelings right now, where do you wrestle the most?

Maybe you wrestle with anger and are known for yelling at your parents or husband when you're upset.

Maybe you struggle with feeling super down when you don't get attention from a certain guy.

Maybe you find yourself constantly irritated at a certain family member or friend and lack all patience.

Maybe you feel stuck in a pit of sadness and don't know how to get out.

Maybe you've been hurt by someone else's sinful choices and are struggling to process your pain.

Maybe deep down you're wrestling with a lot of fear about the future.

Maybe you're grieving over a loss and struggling to see any hope.

Or maybe your tears seem to fall unannounced at the slightest thing.

Emotions are a beautiful and challenging part of life. So, how do we deal with the very real ups and downs of our feelings? How do we walk in truth when everything inside us is screaming to go in the other direction? How do we choose a gracious response when people hurt us? How do we grieve over real loss while still finding our ultimate hope in Christ? How do we find joy when all we feel is numbness?

One of our favorite places to go in the Bible to get help with our emotions is the Psalms. David is the author of many of the Psalms and he's a passionate dude. He's so raw and honest about how he feels. Over and over again, he pours out his heart through the Psalms revealing the highs and lows of his feelings. He experienced so much of what we're feeling today. Check out these verses:

> I am weary with my moaning;
>> every night I flood my bed with tears;
>> I drench my couch with my weeping.
> My eye wastes away because of grief;
>> it grows weak because of all my foes. (Ps. 6:6–7)

> With my voice I cry out to the LORD;
>> with my voice I plead for mercy to the LORD.
> I pour out my complaint before him;
>> I tell my trouble before him. (Ps. 142:1–2)

> O LORD, how many are my foes!
>> Many are rising against me;
> many are saying of my soul,
>> "There is no salvation for him in God."
> But you, O LORD, are a shield about me,
>> my glory, and the lifter of my head.
> I cried aloud to the LORD,
>> and he answered me from his holy hill. (Ps. 3:1–4)

Talk about transparency! It's like David is giving us a peek inside his man journal. He doesn't hesitate to passionately bring his feelings, thoughts, and burdens to the Lord. It's comforting to know that he was a regular human just like us. Notice, though, how he doesn't shove his emotions under the rug or pretend they don't exist. He doesn't vent into thin air either. He takes his feelings to God. He pours out his heart to his Creator.

That's exactly what God wants us to do with our feelings.

Miss Waterworks and the Rock

David's over-the-top expressions of his feelings totally resonate with me (Kristen) because I tend to be a really emotional and passionate person too. When I hit my teen years, I graduated to a new level of emotional drama. I wasn't crying about hamsters and vacuum cleaners anymore, but I was crying about a lot of other things. Bethany began expressing her emotions without as many tears, but I turned into Miss Waterworks herself. We each gained a new nickname from our siblings. They called Bethany "the Rock" (since she rarely cried), and they called me "Miss Waterworks" (no explanation necessary). If I was involved in a conflict, tears were a guarantee. As time went on, Miss Waterworks followed me right into marriage. Hello, Zack.

Several years into my marriage I realized how out of control my emotions had become. I was easily offended by things, assumed the worst, and cried over tiny conflicts. I started praying to God, asking Him to help me gain control over my out-of-control emotions. *Dear God, can You help me zip the lip and dry the cry? Please!*

Several weeks went by, and I didn't notice much change. Then a few days later, I heard a speaker at a Christian conference say something that changed my life forever. They were talking about emotions (of course I attended that session), and they said something to the effect of this: Your emotions are directly fueled by what you think about.

Say whaaaaat?!

My emotions are fueled by what I think?

Bingo! I had been praying for the wrong thing all along. Instead of asking God to help me control my crazy emotions, I needed Him to help me control my *crazy thinking*. It made so much more sense to me. I learned that emotions don't just rise up out of thin air, but rather they're a response to what we're *thinking* about. That's why the Bible talks so much about our minds. About meditating on the truth (*meditation* is just a fancy word for thinking about something over and over again). We're all meditating on something. That's why Ephesians 4:23 calls us to be renewed in the spirit of our minds. Rather than allowing our emotions (good or bad) to steer our lives, we need to step in and redirect our emotions with God's truth.

In the Psalms, we see a pattern of David doing this over and over again. As he's pouring out his heart to God in genuine anguish, he takes things a step further. He doesn't just stop at a place of hopelessness and conclude, "This is really hard, and I'm toast." He intentionally calls to mind God's truth. Let's look at Psalm 3:1–4 again:

> O LORD, how many are my foes!
>   Many are rising against me;
> many are saying of my soul,
>   "There is no salvation for him in God."
>
> *But you*, O LORD, are a shield about me,
>   my glory, and the lifter of my head.
> I cried aloud to the LORD,
>   and he answered me from his holy hill. (emphasis added)

Did you see what he did there? He passionately (and honestly) poured out his fears to the Lord by saying, "Many are rising against me." But then he shifted gears and brought God into the picture. "But you, O Lord, are a shield about me." David was facing real danger, and it was probably terrifying. But in the midst of his fears, he reminded his heart to look to God. He chose to lead his emotions with God's truth.

Another passage that vividly illustrates the need to lead your emotions with truth is Lamentations 3:17–18:

> My soul is bereft of peace;
> I have forgotten what happiness is;
> so I say, "My endurance has perished;
> so has my hope from the Lord."

The writer is clearly overcome with sorrow. There's a sense of weariness and hopelessness. But look at what happens next. It's amazing.

> But this I call to mind,
> and *therefore I have hope*:
> The steadfast love of the Lord never ceases;
> his mercies never come to an end;
> they are new every morning;
> great is your faithfulness.
> "The Lord is my portion," says my soul,
> "therefore I will hope in him."
> The Lord is good to those who wait for him,
> to the soul who seeks him. (Lam. 3:21–25,
> emphasis added)

"But this I call to mind, and therefore I have hope." That's the key. Right there. Calling to mind God's steadfast love . . . then finding hope again. It's incredible! It doesn't mean the circumstances automatically get easier, but the heart isn't hopeless anymore. There is new strength for the challenges ahead.

That is the power of leading our hearts with truth in every area of our lives. Whether it's family relationships, dating, life choices, friendships, work, ministry, grief, anger, jealousy, pain, hurt, or something else, our emotions play a huge role. But our emotions can't be trusted to lead us toward truth, which is why it's crucial for us to guide our feelings with God's truth.

Our good friend Erin Davis explains it this way:

> You may feel like no one loves you when in fact there are dozens of people in your life who care deeply for you. Difficult circumstances may cause you to feel like God has abandoned you when His Word promises that He will never leave you or forsake you (Deut. 31:6). You may even *feel* like a challenge you are facing is impossible to overcome despite the fact that God's Word promises that you can do all things through Christ who strengthens you (Phil. 4:13). The bottom line is, our emotions don't always reflect God's Truth.[1]

Our emotions don't always reflect God's truth.

Exactly. *Our emotions don't always reflect God's truth.* That's why it's so important to intentionally call to mind what is true, so that we can steer our feelings in the right direction.

Lead Your Emotions with Truth

When I (Bethany) was younger, I walked into a restaurant and the hostess behind the counter looked up at me and loudly exclaimed, "Wow! You're freakishly tall!" Yeah, I'm tall for a girl (six foot one), but nobody wants to be called a freak. Especially by a random stranger in public.

In that moment, though, I had a choice to make. How would I process this statement? If I chose to believe the lie that I was a freak, my emotions would follow, leaving me wrecked by insecurity and at odds with my height. But if I chose to reject the lie and believe the truth (i.e., I am fearfully and wonderfully made by God to glorify Him, and my height is a beautiful part of God's design for my body; see Psalm 139:13–17), then my emotions would follow and I would rest confidently in my Creator's design. Thankfully, God helped me to believe the truth in that moment and reject the lie. By God's grace, I refrained from calling her "freakishly short" and went on my way with a smile.

Here are a few other real-life scenarios of what it might look like to lead your feelings with the truth.

Imagine you're lying in your bed at night when you suddenly feel an overwhelming sense of sadness wash over you. You feel alone and unwanted. You feel overlooked and discarded. Your emotions begin spiraling downward. You quickly grab your Bible and turn to Psalms. You read this verse: "For you, O Lord, are my hope, my trust, O Lord, from my youth" (71:5). You begin praying, thanking God for being your true hope. You continue thanking Him for as many blessings (small and big) as you can think of. You praise God for His character. For His love. For His kindness.

For His faithfulness. And before you know it, your heart is a little lighter and a little more hope-filled. You're reminded of how much God loves you.

That, right there, is what it means to lead your emotions with truth.

Or how about this one.

Imagine you're hanging out with your friends and someone makes a sarcastic joke about your outfit being ugly. Inside, you feel hurt and angry. *Why would they say that?* You want to lash out . . . give them a taste of their own medicine. But instead of allowing your angry emotions to lead your decision, you remember the familiar verses that say, "Love is patient and kind; love does not envy or boast; it is not arrogant or rude" (1 Cor. 13:4–5). You say a quick prayer, asking God to help you show kindness in this moment. And then, instead of snapping back with a snarky comment, you choose to respond gently and graciously.

That, right there, is what it means to lead your emotions with truth.

Or how about past hurts that seem to resurface and whisper lies to your heart? Divorce. Abuse. Neglect. Trauma. You feel a deep sense of pain, and rightly so. You should be grieved by brokenness and sin. But these awful memories tend to flood your mind and tell you that you're unlovable. Worthless. Beyond redemption. In your emotional pain, these lies feel compelling. But instead of allowing the darkness to overshadow you, you remind your heart of how much God cares for you. In your grief, you read Psalm 139:13–14, 17–18, which says,

> For you formed my inward parts;
>   you knitted me together in my mother's womb.

I praise you, for I am fearfully and wonderfully made.
Wonderful are your works;
   my soul knows it very well. . . .

How precious to me are your thoughts, O God!
   How vast is the sum of them!
If I would count them, they are more than the sand.
   I awake, and I am still with you.

You allow God's Word to speak truth over the lies, which brings hope to your heart. As you're processing the pain, you're reminded that God loves you deeply and that you're precious to Him. You grieve as someone with hope.

We want to take a quick moment to say this though: If you have experienced any form of abuse or trauma at the hands of another person, we implore you to seek help. Don't walk this journey alone. Seek help from a professional biblically based counselor or a godly mentor who can help you navigate your journey toward healing. And if you're feeling suicidal, please call one of the suicide-prevention hotlines right now (you can find these online). Sister, your life is valuable. Don't give up!

The two of us have seen the power of God working in our hearts and lives as we've brought His truth into the middle of our feelings. We're also happy to report that we no longer cry over vacuum cleaners and hamsters. Our husbands are grateful for that too. However, our childhood nicknames somehow followed us into adulthood. Miss Waterworks and the Rock are still on the scene. To this day, we express our emotions differently as women. And that's okay. We're just grateful that God sees past our roller-coaster mood swings and helps us to lead our emotions with His truth.

We still have a long way to go, but we're encouraged by the progress.

And for the record, we're never buying hamsters again. As cute as they are, we're not interested in putting ourselves through that kind of drama. Hamster farms aren't really our thing.

Ponder IT

Filtering your emotions with truth doesn't mean you ignore your feelings; it means you bring God into your feelings.

Remember

★ God created us with emotions, and He has a good plan for how we can embrace them in the right way.

★ Our emotions don't always reflect God's truth.

★ Instead of being led by our emotions, God wants to help lead our emotions with His truth.

★ What we choose to think about and believe will fuel how we feel.

★ Emotions have their rightful and good place in our lives, but that should always be behind the steering wheel of God's truth.

SHARE YOUR HEART

Dear Lord,

Thank You for creating me with emotions. I'm grateful
for the ability to feel deeply, to love others intimately, to
laugh with joy, and to grieve during hard times. These
emotions are a gift from You, and I praise You for them.
Thank You for hearing my prayers and allowing me
to pour my heart out to You! In my life, I know that my
emotions can get the better of me and lead me down
the wrong path. I know that my heart is quick to dwell on
the wrong things and believe lies rather than Your truth.
Help me to take my thoughts captive to the obedience
of Christ and to lead my emotions with Your Word. Help
me to find my ultimate hope and identity in You.

Amen.

Consider

Psalm 42:1-6

As a deer pants for flowing streams,
    so pants my soul for you, O God.
My soul thirsts for God,
    for the living God.
When shall I come and appear before God?
My tears have been my food
    day and night,
while they say to me all the day long,
    "Where is your God?"

These things I remember,
as I pour out my soul;
how I would go with the throng
and lead them in procession to the house of God
with glad shouts and songs of praise,
a multitude keeping festival.

Why are you cast down, O my soul,
and why are you in turmoil within me?
Hope in God; for I shall again praise him,
my salvation and my God.

DIG DEEPER

Proverbs 4:23

Romans 12:2

Philippians 2:1-11

WHAT ABOUT YOU?

1. Do you remember a funny "crying your eyes out" moment from your childhood?

2. Do you express your emotions more externally (blow up) or more internally (clam up)? Why is that?

3. In what ways have you seen your emotions being directly fueled by your thoughts?

4. What can you learn from the way David poured out his heart to God in the Psalms?

5. If you're walking through a season where your feelings are turning dark, what steps can you take right now to reach out for help?

6. How can you do a better job of bringing God's truth into the midst of your feelings?

Go FOR IT

Here's a fun and practical exercise to help you take your wrong thoughts captive. Grab three sticky notes or small pieces of paper. Next, write the words "What am I thinking about?" on each piece. Now, stick each of the papers at eye level in places where you do a lot of your thinking (e.g., bathroom mirror, headboard of your bed, next to your computer, etc.). For the next week, every time you begin to feel emotional about something, look at that paper and ask yourself, "What am I thinking about?" If your thoughts are going down the wrong path, pause and pray in that moment, asking God to help you think about what is true.

why are you
cast down, O my soul,
and why are you
in turmoil within me?
Hope in God;
for I shall again
praise him,
my salvation
and my God.

Psalm 42:11

chapter 7

Trust the One Who Holds Tomorrow

The two of us snagged a table on the back patio of our favorite local San Antonio coffee shop with hot mochas in hand. (Yes, the crazy mocha ladies are back. See our book *Sex, Purity, and the Longings of a Girl's Heart* for the full story on that one.) Kristen glanced up at me and said out loud what we'd both been thinking over the past several weeks.

"Are we going to do this thing or not? It's kind of like now or never. I'm married, but I don't have kids, and you're single. Our time will probably never be this free again. What do you think?"

Deep in my heart I knew this was it. We'd either put everything we had into launching a ministry together, or we'd forget about our dream and move on in life. I had to admit that the timing did seem perfect. Kristen had been married for a few years but didn't have any kids yet. I was still single as a Pringle. It only made sense that we'd use this unusually open season of our lives to encourage and mentor as many younger girls as possible.

"I think you're right," I said. "It's now or never. I feel like God has us in this unique season for a reason. Maybe He's kept us freed up from other responsibilities so we could pour our time into starting a ministry."

And that was that.

The launch of Girl Defined Ministries.

Circa 2014.

Nothing big. Nothing fancy. Just two sisters trying to use their time wisely and encourage young women in this crazy world we call home. What started out as a do-or-die meeting at the coffee shop turned into the beautiful work that would become an integral part of our lives. From that moment forward, the two of us poured hours of our time into launching a website (www.GirlDefined.com), writing blog posts, filming videos, creating social media posts, and so much more.

Little did we know that we'd go on to write several books, with this big beauty of a book being our fifth. We'd have the opportunity to literally travel the world together sharing about God's amazing design for womanhood with the sisterhood. What a ride. And it's not over yet.

Trusting the Master Artist

Okay, now rewind with us to a few short years before Girl Defined Ministries came into existence. The year was 2011, and as you already know, that was the year Kristen got married to her husband, Zack. And that was the year that I purchased that wedding dress that is still hanging in the back of my closet. At this point in time, we both assumed God would give us the good and, frankly, biblical desires of our hearts (i.e., godly husbands and houses full of adorable children). Little did we know that the absence of those "good" things would become the very reason we were able to start Girl Defined Ministries.

God knew what He was doing.

Yes, we knew that God was trustworthy, but we had no idea where He was taking us. Have you ever felt like that before? That's a hard place to be in. Having no idea where God is leading but fighting to trust that He is the Master Painter, sees the full picture, and will lead you exactly where He wants you to go. Much easier said than done. It's so stinking hard to hand the paintbrush over to God and allow Him to paint the picture He has in mind for your life. This has been a continuous battle for the two of us. We've wanted to grab the paintbrush and start painting the picture that we'd dreamed up for our lives. The cute little house. The white picket fence. The adoring husband. The sweet kids (who never fight, argue, or make messes, of course). Just the basics. Nothing too fancy.

God had a different timeline.

Trusting God became a constant theme for the two of us as we managed Girl Defined Ministries. I (Bethany) remember one instance in particular when this was really hard for me. Kristen and I were working on our very first book, *Girl Defined: God's Radical Design for Beauty, Femininity, and Identity*. It was a particularly hard week of writing. Let me just say that writing does not come easily to me. I'm not even kidding. Every word of *Girl Defined* was a serious labor of love. Forming words on paper (including these words) is just stinking hard for me!

During this challenging season of writing, I remember seeing Zack's loving support for Kristen boost her spirits. I felt like it just wasn't fair. She could finish a hard day of writing and have the loving understanding of her husband to encourage her. I didn't have that. I would finish a long day of writing and go home to no one. Yes, I had my immediate family. But I didn't have *that* person. The person who would have a special interest in my life and care deeply about the nitty-gritty details of what I've been through. The person who would be my shoulder to cry on. My prayer warrior. My teammate. I had my dog, Fluffy, which was great. But not a man. Not my true love.

In those moments of struggle, I cried out to God and asked Him to do the work inside my heart to help me trust Him.

I'm sure you have your own "struggling to trust God right now" moments. Moments when you look at the path before you and wish it looked different. Moments when you glance to your side and wish you had someone to do life with. Moments when you just can't feel God's presence, and you wish He'd make Himself more felt in your life.

> God is the Master Painter, and He has the end *picture* in mind.

As difficult as those moments can be, the answer remains the same. God is the Master Painter, and He has the end picture in mind. He knows where the valleys will be, and He knows where the mountaintop moments will be. He knows that the final masterpiece will be most beautiful if we trust Him with the paintbrush.

So, how exactly do we trust Him with each stroke of our life story? There's a short passage found in Proverbs 3 that has become an anchor in my life. It's literally been my life verse and rock. Let's look at it together:

> Trust in the LORD with all your heart,
>   and do not lean on your own understanding.
> In all your ways acknowledge him,
>   and he will make straight your paths. (vv. 5–6)

Let's dig into each line a little deeper.

"Trust in the LORD *with all your heart."*

God doesn't want part of our heart. He doesn't want the nasty leftovers in the back-left corner of the fridge that are molding. He doesn't want the part that's easiest to give. That's not what this verse is saying. This verse makes it crystal clear that He wants all of it. He wants the full surrender. Why is it so easy to give all our heart to other things, like guys, work, friends, or a television show, but so hard to totally give it to God? I wish it were the other way around. Don't you? By trusting in the Lord with all your heart, you're humbly admitting that God's ways are better. That God is wiser. That His character is perfectly good and loving (which we know it is). That it would be foolish to rely on our own finite wisdom rather than trust our mighty Creator. Trusting in the Lord with all your heart is an act of humility. It's acknowledging how great God is and how very small we are in comparison.

"And do not lean on your own understanding."

That's the contrasting piece to the verse. We are to trust in the Lord with all our heart and not lean on our own understanding. Why? Because our understanding is incredibly limited. We have a teeny-tiny view of life, of this world, and only mere speculation about the future. God sees and knows everything. He knows where we've been and where we're going. Leaning on your own understanding would be like taking the paintbrush from Leonardo da Vinci and asking him to step aside. Yikes! How foolish and silly would that be? It would be crazy! Insane, in fact. And yet, that's what we try to do with God. Not leaning on your own understanding is acknowledging that God is the Master Artist and you are not. It's letting Him paint the portrait of your life.

"In all your ways acknowledge him."

This means acknowledging God in the little things and the big things. It's saying, *God, I'd really love for this relationship with this guy to work out. He seems so awesome, and I think we'd make an amazing couple. Even though I really want this, I'm opening my hands and surrendering this to You. Please give me wisdom. Please help me to listen. Please bring out anything in our relationship that is not honoring or would not be beneficial to him or to me. Please end this if it's not Your plan for me. I trust You. I want Your will.* Acknowledging Him is wanting what God wants long term, not just what you want in the current moment. It's being willing to follow God down a different path than you'd imagined for your life if He makes that clear. Acknowledging God is simply living a surrendered life one day at a time.

"And he will make straight your paths."

This is beautiful. God promises that He will direct your paths if you do the above things He's listed. He will guide you, and He will do it one step at a time. One moment at a time. One day at a time. If you're trusting in Him with all your heart, not leaning on your own understanding, and acknowledging Him in all your ways, you better believe that He absolutely will direct your paths. He won't always direct them where you want Him to direct them. But He will always direct them where He knows is best. Imagine a little toddler who's starting to walk. Toddlers need a lot of guidance and assistance for every next step. If left to themselves, they would most likely end up hurt or somewhere they really don't want to be. We are like the toddler. We need God's guidance for every step of the way. In those moments when you're struggling and want to go your own way, take a deep breath and remind yourself to trust in Him with all your heart.

It's Hard to Trust

Girl, we get it. We get how difficult it is to put this whole trust thing into practice. When life is messy, it's hard to trust. When you thought God was doing one thing, and He closes the door and takes you in a different direction, it's hard to trust. When something happens that's totally outside of your control and you can't fix it, it's hard to trust. When you desperately want God to intervene for you in a certain way and He doesn't, it's hard to trust.

If trusting God were easy, we'd all be doing it.

It's not though. Every single one of us needs God's amazing grace and the power of the Holy Spirit working within us to live this out. We need His help. We need His grace. We need His strength.

When the two of us were sitting at the coffee shop that day, we had no idea where God was going to direct our steps. To be quite honest, we were a little freaked out. Okay, a lot freaked out. It's stinking scary handing over the paintbrush to God. Even though you know He's good, it's still scary. We didn't know if He'd give us our personal dreams of marriage and children. We didn't know how far this ministry thing would go. We had no clue. We just knew that He was calling us to trust in Him with all our hearts, not to lean on our own understanding, to acknowledge Him in all our ways, and to believe that He would direct our steps. We weren't sure if we'd like where He directed us, but we knew that His plan was and is so much better than ours could ever be. We didn't know what the future held, but we knew the One who held our future.

Have you ever been to one of those painting studios with a group of friends? You know, those places where each person gets their own easel and canvas, and the instructor guides them every step of the way? Kristen and I went to one of those a few years ago. It was so humiliating. The teacher continued making extra trips by my canvas to give me tips. I got the hint. My painting was awful. I'm no artist. Painting and I have never worked well together. My picture looked like a three-year-old was let loose with a pack of markers and crayons. I threw that canvas away the moment I got home. I didn't want any of my friends catching sight of that mess.

All in all, it was a good reminder that I was not the teacher or the artist. I can attempt to re-create the masterpiece, but it will always fall short.

To this day, Kristen and I are still on a journey of learning to trust God. You might find yourself on that same journey too. Like so many women we've talked to, we still have unmet desires. We still have prayers we'd love for God to answer in the way we want Him to answer them. Yeah, God. Don't just answer my prayer . . . answer it exactly the way I want it. We still struggle with wanting to lean on our own understanding. We still want things our own way. In all of this, we know the truth though. We know that God is a better artist than da Vinci, van Gogh, and Picasso combined. And He's definitely better than that amateur Bethany Beal. We know it'd be incredibly foolish to take the paintbrush and try to create our own masterpiece. It would be child's play in comparison to the masterpiece He is working on. He is creating a masterpiece out of our story and yours. And the more we learn to trust Him throughout the journey, the more enjoyable the ride will be.

Here's a simple tool that has been helpful for us in understanding how to trust God more fully.

> He is creating a *masterpiece* out of our story and yours.

Do you see the two circles on the next page? The smaller circle is filled with areas where God is calling us, as Christians, to trust and obey Him right now. These are areas of obedience He's calling us to walk in. And this list is just a start. You can search online for "commands of Christ," and you'll see exactly what Christ commanded in the New Testament. Or take a look in the Bible at Matthew 4 and 5. You will find a bunch in there as well. These commands are so helpful and offer such clear guidance for us. Whenever you wonder what you're supposed to be doing in your life or where God is leading you, stop and ask yourself if you're walking in obedience to God's instruction for you as a Christian.

Do you see the larger circle? Those are the things God is calling us to entrust to Him and pray about. We don't know what God's plan is for us in those areas. The answers aren't written for us in Scripture. The Bible doesn't say, "On October 14, 2018, Bethany Baird will marry David Beal." Yes, God knew that, but I (Bethany) did not. That was an area of trust for me.

How much easier would it be to trust God if we knew what the future held, right? But only God knows the future. God is omniscient (all-knowing), and we are not. This is why we must entrust these things to Him through prayer.

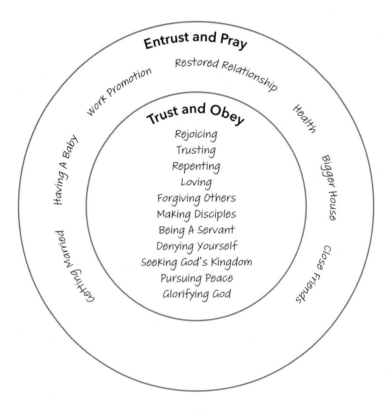

There are two additional circles below. These are for you to personalize and make your own. We want you to take a minute to reflect on your own life.

The smaller circle is for you to write all the areas where you know (according to Scripture) God is calling you to trust and obey Him right now.

The larger circle is for you to write all the areas of your life that you must entrust to God right now. The areas you'd love for God to bring clarity and direction to, change the circumstances of, or make a reality in your life. These are the areas in which you desperately need God's strength to help you trust Him with your future.

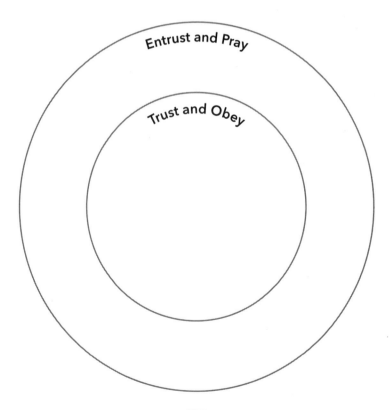

Slow down for a minute and think about that thing that keeps popping into your mind. That thing you so desperately want to hold with a clenched fist. That thing you so desperately want to control and have clear answers for.

Do you have that one thing in mind?

That is the very thing God is specifically calling you to entrust to Him right now. God cares so much about this area of your life. Even though it may not feel like it, He is a good God and He does good. Yes, even in your life. You are not the exception. Entrust that very important thing into the loving hands of God, and watch Him bring peace and rest into your heart.

The two of us believe that God has a good work for you to do (Eph. 2:10). We believe that He has you here for a good purpose (Gal. 6:9). We are cheering you on as you strive to trust God and thrive right where He's planted you. We are praying that you will choose to be faithful. Choose to obey. Choose to trust Him.

God is the Master Painter. As you seek to faithfully trust Him with every stroke of your story, you will one day look back and see the beautiful masterpiece He painted for His glory. We pray that you will open up your hands and release the paintbrush to your Savior.

He is the Perfect Artist.

Ponder IT

> **God is the Master Painter. One day you will be able to look back and see the beautiful masterpiece He painted with your life for His glory.**

Remember

* ✶ Trusting God with all your heart is something He calls every single one of us to do.

* ✶ Trusting God acknowledges that He is in control.

* ✶ If trusting God were easy, we'd all be doing it.

* ✶ When you trust in the Lord with all your heart, you're humbly admitting that God's ways are better than yours.

* ✶ Obey God in the areas He's already laid out for you in Scripture.

* ✶ God is the Master Painter, and He has the end picture in mind. He knows that the final masterpiece will be most beautiful if He is trusted with the paintbrush.

SHARE **YOUR HEART**

Dear Lord,

Why is trusting You so hard? Why do I desperately want to snatch the paintbrush and create my own story?

Please help me. I know You're the Master Artist. I know Your ways are better than my ways. Help me to keep my eyes on You as I take one step after another. The path is dark, and I can barely see what's in front of me. I don't know what tomorrow holds or the next day or the next. But You do. I trust that You have me in the family, the church, the community, the school, and the job I'm in for a reason. Please help me to live for Your glory right where You have me. I trust that You will direct my steps for tomorrow. Help me to be faithful today.

Amen.

Consider

Proverbs 3:5-8

Trust in the LORD with all your heart,
    and do not lean on your own understanding.
In all your ways acknowledge him,
    and he will make straight your paths.
Be not wise in your own eyes;
    fear the LORD, and turn away from evil.
It will be healing to your flesh
    and refreshment to your bones.

Jeremiah 17:7-8

Blessed is the man who trusts in the LORD,
    whose trust is the LORD.
He is like a tree planted by water,
    that sends out its roots by the stream,

and does not fear when heat comes,
    for its leaves remain green,
and is not anxious in the year of drought,
    for it does not cease to bear fruit.

DIG DEEPER

Psalm 28:7   Proverbs 29:25

Psalm 56:3-4   Romans 15:13

Proverbs 3

WHAT ABOUT YOU?

1. Why do you think trusting God is difficult for most of us?

2. What is one area of your life that you're struggling to trust God with right now?

3. How did the circle tool change your perspective of trusting God?

4. Why is it silly to try to direct your own steps and paint your own story?

5. Reread Proverbs 3:5-8. In what ways does this passage bring you hope?

Go
FOR IT If you haven't filled out the circle
tool, go ahead and do that right now. Once you're
done, look through everything that's listed inside
each circle. Choose one thing from each circle and
write them on the lines below. Spend a few minutes in
prayer.

Ask God to specifically help you to trust and obey
Him in the area that He's already commanded in
Scripture. Next, ask God to help you entrust this per-
sonal area of your life into His loving care.

_____

_____

And those who
know your name
put their *trust*
in you, for you,
O LORD,
have not forsaken
those who
seek you.

Psalm 9:10

chapter 8

Freed Up to Live for Him

I (Bethany) started attending a church in the quaint little town of Fredericksburg, Texas, when I was in my early twenties. This was a huge change for me. Up to this point, I'd been attending the same well-established church my entire life in San Antonio. That's around 1,200 Sundays sitting on the same church pew and staring at the same old wooden podium. Although switching to this small-town church was a stretch for me, it seemed like the right decision due to some structural changes happening at my old church. What I didn't know then was that God was weaving together a beautiful love story for me, and this small country church is where it would all begin.

I'll never forget the first time I pulled up to this picture-perfect white country church. Little did I know that when I walked through the large cherry-stained wooden front doors, I would lay eyes on my future husband for the very first time.

In the spirit of total honesty, this wasn't a romantic first meeting. It definitely wasn't love at first sight, though I wish it had been. Doesn't every girl secretly hope for that? I was twenty-three, and he was about seventeen years old (yeah, it would have been kind of an illegal relationship at that moment). He was basically still a boy, and I was a full-grown woman. I had zero clue that this teenage guy, David Jonathan Beal, would grow up and, seven years later, become my husband and the father of my children.

The next several years passed, and I had very minimal interaction with David. To be honest, he wasn't even really a friend. More like an acquaintance at best. Actually, more like my younger brother's friend (yes, I'm that girl who eventually married her younger brother's friend).

During those years of knowing David (but not really knowing him on a personal level), I went through another serious relationship, experienced another breakup, and continued to wrestle with my singleness. I wondered if God had a plan for me, and I struggled to live a surrendered life. Although I couldn't (still can't) see the future, God knew what He was up to. He was working big-time in my life, and He was working big-time in David's life as well. God was molding us, shaping us, and truly preparing us for each other.

We just didn't know it yet.

From my mid to late twenties, I felt like God was pruning my heart and trying to teach me to live all out for Him. I have a distinct memory of sitting on my bed and wondering what in the world I was doing with my life. I remember pulling my knees to my chest and just bawling my eyes out. My life didn't look at all like I'd planned, and I was struggling to surrender that ideal dream to God.

After a ton of prayer, hours upon hours of soaking my mind in Scripture, and moments of straight-up crying out to God, I came to this realization: my purpose on this earth isn't to fulfill my dreams for my life.

I'm not here to make my name great.

I'm not here to get all the things I want.

I'm not here to gain accolades or praise.

I'm not here to build up my own kingdom.

I'm here to bring glory to God and point others to Him (Matt. 5:16).

I realized that whether I was single or married, my purpose remained the same. *Glorify God.* Yes, if I got married, my circumstances would change, but my life's aim as a daughter of God would remain the same.

That thought was incredibly freeing to me.

It was during those years of knowing David but not really knowing him that God changed my heart and helped me to live a truly surrendered life. A life that was surrendered to God and His Word. A life that was willing to give up anything (even my dream of marriage) in order to glorify my Savior.

It sounds crazy to say, but the more I surrendered my life to God, the more I thrived. The more I viewed myself as an ambassador for Christ, the more excitement I felt about my future. The more I understood that my life was all about God, the more satisfying my life became. The more I focused on living for Jesus, the more I loved my life. The more I lived out my purpose to bring glory to God, the more purpose I had in every little detail of my life.

Okay with Never Getting Married

It was through this time of surrendering that I became 100 percent okay with the idea of never getting married. Yes, I was still hopeful about marriage and desired it, but it wasn't a must-have for me. I genuinely wanted to live all out for Christ, and I wanted to do that in whatever way God saw fit. If that meant being single forever, great. If that meant getting married and serving God alongside my husband, great.

Coming to a place of complete surrender is what God wants for each of us.

So how do we get there? How do we live a fully surrendered life?

The first step of surrender starts with the basics. It starts with trusting in Jesus for your salvation (Rom. 10:9–10). It starts with accepting Him as your Savior and believing that He is who He says He is: the Savior of the world. If that's not something you've done yet, I encourage you to slow down and start there. Everything else I'm about to share with you is meaningless if you haven't made that personal decision to trust in Christ for your eternal salvation. I encourage you to open up a Bible to the book of John. This is a wonderful book in Scripture to help you better understand that decision.

If you have made that decision to trust Jesus for salvation, I have a question for you: What's keeping you from living a fully surrendered life to Him right now? What's keeping you from following the example of Jesus and saying, "Not my will, but yours, be done" (Luke 22:42)? This is the place of surrender I want for you and for me. Here's what living a surrendered life might look like for you. See which one resonates with your heart right now.

God, I desire marriage so much; however, not my will, but Yours, be done.

God, I'd love to get into that school; however, not my will, but Yours, be done.

God, I'd love to have children; however, not my will, but Yours, be done.

God, I'd love to adopt one day; however, not my will, but Yours, be done.

God, I'd love to have my own place right now; however, not my will, but Yours, be done.

God, I'd love to get that promotion; however, not my will, but Yours, be done.

God, I'd love to serve on the mission field overseas; however, not my will, but Yours, be done.

God, please help me with that scholarship; however, not my will, but Yours, be done.

God, change my circumstances; however, not my will, but Yours, be done.

God, please, please answer this prayer; however, not my will, but Yours, be done.

Not my *will*, but Yours, be done. Yours be done in every area of my *life*.

That is what the surrendered life is all about. It's genuinely saying to God, Not my will, but Yours, be done. Yours be done in every area of my life. Big and small. I want Your will in my relationships. In my marriage. In my fertility. In my career. In my education. In my finances. In my dreams. In my ambitions. And absolutely everywhere else. The surrendered life is focused on serving God in and through everything you do.

This was the place of surrender that God brought me to several years ago. When I got to this place of surrender, I just remember feeling so free. I finally felt free to live for God with no other agenda standing in the way. That heart of surrender and life of freedom is exactly what God wants for you too.

My Unexpected Path toward Marriage

Four years had passed from the time I met that David guy from church. Let's just say that a few years can bring some big changes in a person's life. David went from being a skinny teenage boy to being quite the handsome man in his twenties.

Goodbye boy, hello *man*!

To my pleasant surprise, David started showing up. He started showing up at events I was attending. He started showing up at group hangs with friends. He even started showing up at parties my family was hosting at their house (thanks to my brother for inviting him). I wasn't exactly looking for a romantic relationship, but I couldn't help but notice this grown-up version of a guy I'd once seen at church.

When David was at an event or party, everyone knew it. He was full of joy. Full of life. Full of hilarious humor. Everyone loved being around him, including me.

Without even realizing it, I found myself starting to admire this guy. Okay, I started crushing on him (*admire* just sounded more mature). I'll admit it. I started noticing him and wanting to be around him. I found myself looking forward to seeing him. I found myself thinking about him when I wasn't with him. I found myself wondering if he might be interested in me too. Have you ever been in a situation like that? You know, that feeling of torment when you like a guy, and you have no idea if he's interested in you too? It's the worst.

This blossoming friendship with David quickly became an area of internal conflict for me. I wanted to serve God wherever He took me in life, but I wasn't sure if David was a part of that plan. I didn't want to get distracted by this amazing guy if he wasn't a part of God's plan for my future. I even started asking God to take away my feelings for David. Ever been there? But then I also started praying that David would like me if that was God's will. I started to feel jealous when other girls interacted with David (I know you can relate to this one). All in all, I was becoming a small hot mess. I found my heart so drawn toward this man and yet so confused at the same time.

I wondered why God brought this guy into my life.

I had finally come to the place where I was thriving in my singleness. I was serving God wholeheartedly. Why was I allowing myself to be distracted by this guy? I tried to stop. But my efforts were futile. The more I tried to stop liking this guy, the more I liked him. My heart was in turmoil.

A few months into this crush situation, I found myself away from home on vacation in the mountains. The timing was perfect. I needed to clear my head. I needed to get some perspective. I took advantage of this time away from my friends . . . away from David . . . to refocus on God and re-surrender my life to Him. I spent hours journaling, praying, and just begging God to remove the feelings I had for David. I didn't want this distraction in my life if it was just a dead-end road. Ultimately, I chose to trust God with the entire situation. I prayed, *Not my will, but Yours, be done!*

Too soon, I had to give up the fresh mountain air and return home to the scorching Texas heat.

I couldn't help but notice that something was different. David was different. Absence makes the heart grow fonder . . . I guess? David's heart seemed fonder toward me. I noticed his quick responses to my messages. His lingering smiles across the room. His special focused attentiveness to my needs. His wanting to be near me. Something was different. He was treating me differently than he treated any other girl. My heart was swooning. I was liking where this was going.

And then it happened.

The day I secretly hoped for, but never imagined would actually come, actually came. David called me on the phone and asked me to dinner. My crush asked me on a date! I had been praying about this guy for months. I knew without a shadow of a doubt that I wanted to go on this date. I wasn't sure if there would be a date number two, but I knew I needed to at least go on this first one. I wanted to see if there was enough connection to give us a reason to go out again. I wanted to see if God had something in store for us.

Long story short, the first date went better than I could have dreamed. We had a blast together. We encouraged one another. We inspired one another. I felt like David was someone I wanted to get to know in a deeper and more personal way.

He asked me out on a second date. A third date. A fourth date. And countless more.

After several months of dating, it was crystal clear that we were better together. We pushed each other toward Christ and helped each other love God more fully. As much as I'd surrendered my future dream of marriage to God and learned to thrive in my singleness, I knew God was changing my direction.

My purpose of glorifying God would remain the same, but my circumstances and marital status were going to change.

A few days before we got engaged, we both wrote about our feelings in our journals. Here's a sneak peek into what we each said.

BETHANY'S JOURNAL

May 24, 2018

Oh. My. Word. I think I'm getting engaged on Saturday. Dāv wants me to wear a cute dress, and he's picking me up at 10:30 a.m. I am beyond thrilled, and I will say "yes" for sure! There is no doubt in my mind that he is the one. I love this man with all of my heart. I can't wait to be his wife. Bethany Beal. I'm so ready.

DAVID'S JOURNAL

May 25, 2018

I am absolutely FREAKING OUT!!! Tomorrow is the day I propose to Bethany Lynn Baird. I am so excited, I'm almost crying. She has grown to mean more to me than anyone ever has. She 100 percent has my heart forever. I will always love her. I'm just so grateful. Lord, why do I get to be with her?! She is beyond anything I ever will deserve.

DAVID'S JOURNAL

May 27, 2018

On May 26, 2018, at about 2:20 p.m., I proposed to Bethany, and she said, "Of course!" We are now an engaged couple! I could not be more thrilled and excited! God is so wonderful to give me a relationship with such an amazing angel! I LOVE BETHANY SO, SO MUCH!

New Journey, Same Purpose

That was only the beginning of our journey together. God was so gracious to give us each other as best friends, lovers, and teammates for life. On October 14, 2018, we made a covenant before God, family, and friends to honor and love each other until death do us part. Walking down the aisle to David was a dream I never imagined would become my reality. I remember feeling overwhelmed with excitement and awe. This was actually happening. It was MY wedding day. I wasn't a guest or a bridesmaid. I was the bride! And for the record, I didn't end up wearing that "dream" dress hanging in the back of my closet. More on that later.

Everything about our wedding day was perfect. Okay, minus the fact that it felt like a million degrees outside in Texas, and we were all dripping with sweat and completely disgusting by the end of the night. David and I didn't care a bit though. It was our wedding day. We were married. Sweat and all.

Since that day, marriage has changed my life in so many ways. It has impacted almost everything I do. It has also given me the opportunity to love and serve in ways I couldn't as a single woman. I now have a husband I am called to honor and respect. Everything else is no longer "mine," it's "ours," from finances to schedules to future plans. I have someone else who takes top priority in my life.

As much as I love being married and love the ever-living daylights out of my husband, he isn't my number-one priority.

That might sound weird to some of you. Others of you may be thinking, *Go girl! You are number one!* That's not what I mean though. I'm not my number one. My husband isn't my number one. As cheesy as this sounds, God truly is my number one.

Living a life surrendered to God means that He comes above anyone and everything in life. Whether we're single, married, with children, without, retired, or anything else, the purpose of each of our lives should be to glorify God.

> Living a life *surrendered* to God means that He comes above anyone and *everything* in life.

Let's remind ourselves of God's calling for us as His redeemed daughters. These verses are the essence of what it means to live a surrendered life. This is the epitome of what it means to be a Christian.

Seek First the Kingdom of God

But seek first the kingdom of God and his righteousness, and all these things will be added to you. (Matt. 6:33)

Seek the Approval of God

For am I now seeking the approval of man, or of God? Or am I trying to please man? If I were still trying to please man, I would not be a servant of Christ. (Gal. 1:10)

Love God with All Your Heart

And he said to him, "You shall love the Lord your God with all your heart and with all your soul and with all your mind." (Matt. 22:37)

Remember, You Are the Lord's

For if we live, we live to the Lord, and if we die, we die to the Lord. So then, whether we live or whether we die, we are the Lord's. (Rom. 14:8)

Even Jesus Came to Serve Others

For even the Son of Man came not to be served but to serve, and to give his life as a ransom for many. (Mark 10:45)

Is there anything keeping you from opening your hands and fully surrendering your hopes and dreams to God? For me, singleness was that thing that held me back. It took me years to finally open up my clenched fists and surrender my future dreams of marriage to God. Once I finally learned to love God fully and to live for Him wholeheartedly, I began to thrive.

What is that thing for you? What's clenched in your fists? Is it your relationship status? Maybe your dreams of having children? Is it the changes you wish your husband would make? Maybe it's your parents' relationship with one another? What about that promotion you've been wanting? What's keeping you from finally unclenching your fists, surrendering that desire to God, and living fully right now? Right where He has you?

That, my sister, is the surrendered life.

It's living life with the end goal not to get or do what you want but to point others to Jesus. The circumstances of your life will change throughout the years, but your purpose remains the same. *Glorify God.*

When I made that shift and finally surrendered my future to God, I was so free. I was free to serve God, and I didn't need my circumstances to change in order to do that. As wonderful and beautiful as it was to get married, I didn't need marriage in order to thrive. I love my husband dearly. I'm beyond grateful for him. But my purpose of serving and glorifying God is the foundation of who I am. The beauty of the Christian life is that we get to take that purpose with us into every new season we enter.

Whatever season of life you're in right now, you can wholeheartedly live out your beautiful purpose of glorifying God. I encourage you to follow Jesus's example and choose to say, *Not my will, but Yours, be done.* The more you live your life for God's purposes (and not your own), the more you will thrive. What a beautiful life that would be. Free. Free to serve God. Free to love others. Free to thrive exactly where you are today.

That is the beauty of the surrendered life.

Ponder IT

> The surrendered life is focused on serving God throughout every season.

Remember

✷ You're here to bring glory to God and point others to Him.

✷ The surrendered life says, *Not my will, but Yours, be done.*

★ Living a life surrendered to God means that He comes above anyone and everything in life. Whether we're single, married, with children, without, retired, or anything else, the purpose of each of our lives should be to glorify God.

★ Ask God to change you from the inside out. Ask Him to give you the power to live fully surrendered to Him.

SHARE YOUR HEART

"*Lord,*

I give up my own plans and purposes, all my own desires, hopes and ambitions, and I accept Thy will for my life. I give up myself, my life, my all, utterly to Thee, to be Thine Forever. I hand over to Thy keeping all of my friendships; all the people whom I love are to take second place in my heart. Fill me now and seal me with Thy Spirit. Work out Thy whole will in my life at any cost, for to me to live is Christ.

Amen."

—Betty Scott Stam[1]

Consider

1 Peter 4:7-11 NIV

The end of all things is near. Therefore be alert and of sober mind so that you may pray. Above all, love each other deeply, because love covers over a multitude of sins. Offer hospitality to one another without grumbling. Each of you should use whatever gift you have received to serve others, as faithful stewards of God's grace in its various forms. If anyone speaks, they should do so as one who speaks the very words of God. If anyone serves, they should do so with the strength God provides, so that in all things God may be praised through Jesus Christ. To him be the glory and the power for ever and ever. Amen.

DEEPER

Romans 14:8	Ephesians 2:1-10
Galatians 2:20	Philippians 2:5-8
Galatians 5:13	Colossians 3:23-24

WHAT ABOUT YOU?

1. When you hear the word *surrender*, what's the first thing that comes to mind?

2. What is the most important step of surrendering (think salvation)? Have you taken this step? If not, what is it that's keeping you from trusting Jesus as your Savior?

3. Why is Jesus the perfect example of the surrendered life?

4. What's one thing in your life right now that you know you need to surrender?

5. Pull out your Bible and read Matthew 6:33. What does this passage say about seeking?

6. What changes do you need to make in order for Jesus to be number one in your heart?

Go FOR IT Grab your phone or computer and look up the song "I Surrender All" (Phil Wickham has a beautiful version). Find a quiet place where you can listen to this song without distractions. Play the song and let the words wash over your soul. After you've listened to it once, play it a second time. This time make it your prayer to God. Ask God to make the words you're hearing the cry of your heart.

But seek first the *kingdom* of God and his righteousness, and all these things will be added to you.

Matthew 6:33

chapter 9

Sometimes You Laugh, Sometimes You Cry

(Kristen) stared down in shock at the positive pregnancy test in my hands. It had been more than five years since I had seen those double lines. After my two miscarriages early in my marriage, I wondered if I would ever conceive again. For six years I prayed for a baby. I was hopeful. But as each year slowly ticked by, my diagnosis of unexplained infertility loomed like a mysterious fog that wouldn't lift.

But here I was.

Standing in my bathroom on a warm April afternoon, I held the most unexpected news in my hands. I was pregnant. Against all odds, I had conceived again. Zack and I were only a few months away from celebrating our eight-year anniversary, and this news felt like a special gift from the very hand of God.

I felt a surge of joy and excitement pulse through my body. But just as quickly, I felt a wave of fear and anxiety wash over my heart. *What if this pregnancy doesn't work out? What if I miscarry again? What if I share this news with my family only to watch them mourn another loss with me?*

My heart felt like a tornado of emotions.

I wanted to embrace the joy of this miraculous news, but I was deeply afraid to celebrate. As I stared back at myself in the mirror, a calming peace quieted my heart. The words of Psalm 138:8 came to mind and reminded me of this life-giving truth: "The LORD will fulfill his purpose for me; your steadfast love, O LORD, endures forever."

The outcome of my story was not in my hands but in God's. God was in control. He allowed this pregnancy to take place, and He would carry me through whatever path He called me to walk down. Whether joy or sorrow, God was with me. He was in charge of my story. My job was to follow Him and trust Him.

The following days slowly crept by during the initial few weeks of my pregnancy. Every new morning felt like a victory lap. My doctor asked me to come in for weekly appointments since my pregnancy was considered high risk. At my eight-week appointment, my eyes filled with joyful tears as I saw the precious little heartbeat pulsing on the screen. I squeezed Zack's hand as we both looked at the little beating miracle before us. Neither of my first two pregnancies made it past six and a half weeks.

This appointment felt like a milestone victory. My doctor told me to be encouraged. The heartbeat was strong, and the baby was measuring right on track. I couldn't believe this was happening. I allowed myself to dream, for just a second, of what it would be like to actually carry this pregnancy full term. Looking down at my precious ultrasound pictures, I silently prayed, *Please, God. Protect this little life inside of me.*

The weeks slowly continued to tick by. Nothing seemed out of the ordinary. Then I hit week eleven. I began to experience some light bleeding. I grabbed my computer and researched like a crazy lady. The opinions were mixed. This could be serious, or this could be nothing. I decided to schedule an extra appointment with my doctor to check things out. My heart was torn between fear and hope as I walked into her office. *Please, God. Please.*

My doctor greeted me warmly and reassured me that everything was probably fine. As she conducted the ultrasound, her demeanor suddenly changed. She got quiet as she observed the screen. Then, without looking at me, she softly said, "I'm so sorry, honey, but there's no longer a heartbeat."

Her words stabbed me in the chest.

My mind went still.

But I'm eleven weeks along!

Lying on my back, I stared at the ceiling in silence, gripping Zack's hand. Silent tears streamed down my face. I didn't want to believe what I was hearing. This pregnancy was supposed to work out. This was the miracle that was supposed to have a happy ending. This shocking news wasn't part of the plan.

I had no words to speak. All I could do was cry.

After Zack and I slowly made our way out of the office, down the stairs, and into the parking lot, I lost it. The floodgates opened. I cried one of the hardest cries that I had in years. I didn't care who saw me. I was overcome with grief.

Zack pulled me into a tight hug and we cried together. We stood there sobbing in the parking lot until we couldn't cry anymore. Zack took the rest of the day off of work as we grieved the loss of another baby.

The next few days were even harder as we told our family and friends. Everyone was devastated. Even though we received incredible support and love from those around us, the world felt bleak. I knew theologically that God was my hope . . . but I didn't feel hopeful. Not at all. The worst part about this loss was that I didn't miscarry right away. After I received the news that my baby's heartbeat had stopped, it took seven days for me to actually miscarry naturally. Those seven days were like an emotional nightmare. Then, right as my pregnancy app congratulated me for hitting the twelve-week mark, the miscarriage happened.

In the midst of this pain and grief, the story took another unexpected turn.

Just when I thought things couldn't get any harder for me, they did. Exactly one week after my miscarriage took place, Bethany found out she was pregnant. With tears spilling down her face, she shared her news with me. "I'm so sorry," she said with a heavy heart. "We would never have planned it this way."

What was supposed to be one of the happiest moments in her life was a mix of joy and grief for both of us. As you can imagine, this was a challenging moment to navigate as sisters. We loved each other deeply. We cared about each other's lives. We wanted nothing but good for the other person. But how were we going to walk through this? How were we going to love one another well as our paths took polar-opposite directions? Was it even possible to grieve and celebrate at the same time?

I'm sure you can *feel* the tension between us as sisters, even as you're reading this. We had never faced this sort of sensitive and deeply raw dynamic in our relationship until now. We didn't know what to do . . . or how to move forward. Maybe you've been there yourself. If you've been in a position where someone you loved received the very same blessing that you lost, you know how gut-wrenchingly hard it is to navigate. You know how painfully difficult it is to genuinely love that other person while you're facing your own sorrows and loss. It's painful on every level.

For me, the news of Bethany's pregnancy felt like an extra jab in my pain. Not because I didn't want her to be pregnant but because her pregnancy constantly reminded me of my loss. I cried behind closed doors and asked God why. Why would He take this baby from me? Why would He allow my sister to get pregnant at such a sensitive time? Why did He write my story this way? You've probably asked God those very same *why* questions. As we cry out to God in our pain and heartbreak, not only are we desperate for answers . . . but we just want God to put the broken pieces back together and make everything okay again.

The Weight of Grief

I had never experienced grief like *this* before. It was so personal. So overwhelming. So unavoidable. I wanted to escape the pain but had nowhere to run. I felt spiritually numb for a while and wondered if I would ever experience joy again. The answers never came audibly. But over the next few months, God comforted my heart in ways that only He could. It was during this trying season that He lovingly took me to a new level of dependence on Him. As I turned to His Word for strength, I was reminded again that "the LORD will fulfill his purpose for me; your steadfast love, O LORD, endures forever" (Ps. 138:8).

I clung to these words like a lifeline. I had nothing else to cling to. In the midst of my pain, loss, brokenness, and unanswered questions, I knew God had a greater purpose for my loss. And in that greater purpose, I knew that He loved me deeply.

> I knew God had a greater *purpose* for my loss. And in that greater purpose, I knew that He *loved* me deeply.

As Bethany's pregnancy progressed, we both tried our hardest to support one another. I would be lying if I said that every moment was a piece of cake though. Some days were a lot harder than others. Some days I would just cry out of sadness for what could have been. And some days I would cry for the baby that I never got to hold. Other days I would just cry and cry, wishing I was still pregnant. Over time, the weight of the grief began to lighten up a little. The initial gut-punch feeling of shock was over, and I was able to process reality a little better.

Around the two-month mark after my miscarriage, I decided to share the news of my loss online. This was hard and healing. Sharing personal losses online isn't for everyone, and it may not be for you. But for me, I wanted to create a bridge for healing conversations with other women who had experienced similar losses. Shortly after posting, I began getting message after message from sweet Christian sisters around the world asking how I was doing. Since so much of my life and Bethany's are lived publicly online through Girl Defined Ministries, people saw what was going on. They genuinely wanted to know how we were doing as sisters.

I knew I needed to talk openly about this. I wanted to be transparent about my own journey while also offering hope to anyone wrestling with a similar tension. God was working in my life and teaching me that grief and joy can coexist in the same heart at the same time. God was helping me see that I could mourn the loss of my own baby and, at the same time, rejoice over my sister's pregnancy. Here's a snippet of what I shared online during that time:

> Although my heart breaks for my own loss, my heart does not break for my sister's joy.
>
> One thing that God has been pressing into my heart is that I can weep and rejoice at the same time. I have the freedom to grieve my loss while at the same time celebrate my sister's joy. With Christ's strength working in us, I believe it is possible for all of us to do that at the same time. We don't have to live exclusively in one camp or the other.
>
> As Romans 12:15 so beautifully reminds us, "Rejoice with those who rejoice, weep with those who weep." Over the past few months, I have been encouraged by so many amazing godly sisters (online and in person) who are living this verse out with so much grace and love. Many of you have been supporting me 100% with your prayers and sympathy while at the same time supporting Bethany 100% with cheers and congratulations.
>
> This is what it means to live inside both camps. We weep with those who weep and rejoice with those who rejoice. With Christ's strength, we can embrace our own seasons of disappointment while simultaneously celebrating with

those who receive the very blessings we desire. I believe this is what God calls us to embrace as Christian sisters, and it's a beautiful thing to behold.[1]

My words were met with an overwhelming response of understanding and encouragement. I heard from so many women who shared how they were walking in a similar tension in their own lives. Some shared that they were single and longing for marriage while struggling to celebrate their best friend's engagement. Some were walking through the loss of a job while their own siblings seemed to easily climb the ladder of success. Others wrestled with disappointment when they didn't see their prayers being answered, but the prayers of those closest to them were. Some also shared how they were walking through the pain of miscarriage while everyone around them seemed to get pregnant with every sneeze.

As my heart ached for hope and encouragement, I saw the same longing in countless other women. We were each walking through our own unique story of sorrow and joy. We were each wrestling with our own losses while living in the midst of other people's blessings. As we dialogued about this online, we found strength in one another's stories. God was working. He wasn't done with us yet.

And, sister, God isn't done with you either.

Learning to Weep and Rejoice

Although I may not know you personally (or maybe I do!), we already share something big in common. We're each facing, have already faced, or will face loss, disappointment, and grief in our life. If we don't know how to get through these trials while living among our family and friends, how will we survive? How will we thrive? Here's what else we both have in common: sister, we both have to learn what it means to live in the tension of Romans 12:15, which says, "Rejoice with those who rejoice, weep with those who weep." We have to learn how to weep over our very real losses in healthy ways while also rejoicing with the people we love. Hard? Yes! Impossible? Not with God's help.

I'll be honest with you and say that I was very tempted to get mad at Bethany after my miscarriage. I was tempted to view her blessing as a direct attack on my loss. Ever felt that way toward a family member or friend? It's a strange blend of emotions, right? But here's the truth for my situation and for yours: their blessing has nothing to do with our loss. God's plans are unique for each one of us. His purposes stretch beyond what we can see.

As I grieved my own loss (which is a healthy and good thing to do), I made room in my heart to celebrate my sister's joy. I knew that the way I responded to this challenging circumstance would lay the foundation for the next year. I had a hard choice to make. I could either choose the path of anger, resentment, and bitterness (toward God and Bethany), or I could choose the path of joy, gratitude, and genuine celebration.

By God's grace, I chose the latter.

I knew that a bitter heart wouldn't get me to a better place. I knew that harboring resentment would only steal my joy. I knew that anger wouldn't produce any solutions. As Proverbs 14:10 says, "The heart knows its own bitterness, and no stranger shares its joy."

So, in the days, weeks, and months following my miscarriage, I genuinely cried out to God, asking Him to help me make the daily choice to love my sister. To celebrate her joys. To rejoice in her blessings. But even more than that, I asked God for the daily strength to trust Him. To trust His sovereign plan. To trust His timing. To trust His ways.

Over time, through this process, some major healing happened in my heart. And friend, this is exactly what God wants for you too. Healing and hope can be your reality as you choose to take daily baby steps of trusting God, rejoicing with others, and fervently praying. It's forward motion: intentionally choosing to put one foot (spiritually, emotionally, and physically) in front of the other.

As I did this, I began to see, firsthand, why the Bible says, "It is more blessed to give than to receive" (Acts 20:35). Not only is it more blessed because of the joy we receive in the giving (although that's a wonderful thing), I think it's more blessed because *giving* is at the very heart of who God is.

> *Serving* and loving others is at the very *core* of our Savior's character.

Jesus, the very Son of God, came to this earth "not to be served but to serve, and to give his life as a ransom for many" (Matt. 20:28). Serving and loving others is at the very core of our Savior's character.

As you walk through seasons when this feels very hard to do, remind your heart of who Jesus is. Remind your heart of your bigger mission to love others and point them back to their Savior. Here's what this looks like:

When you pour out your *love* for others, you become more like Jesus.

When you choose to *give* when everything in you is screaming to shut down, hide, and retreat, you display a compelling picture of sacrificial love.

When you *serve*, you put the gospel on display through your actions.

When you *celebrate* what God is doing in the lives of others, you point them back to the real Giver of those good gifts.

When you genuinely *show up* for someone who received the very blessing you desire, you're tangibly reminding them that God is good and can be trusted with the details of our lives.

Sister, this is why it's more blessed to give than to receive.

We become tangible vessels of Jesus's love to those around us.

We receive the joy of Christ in our hearts as we follow in His footsteps.

In our emptiness, Christ fills us up as we pour out for others.

Although your life circumstances aren't exactly the same as mine, these truths apply to your life in the same way.

Maybe your struggle is similar to what Bethany wrestled with for many years. You long to get married and have that special someone by your side, but God isn't answering your prayers in the way you'd hoped. You're struggling to celebrate the joys of your family and friends who are getting married all around you. The wedding showers, bachelorette parties, rehearsal dinners, and wedding ceremonies are grating on your nerves. Sister, this is right where God wants to meet you.

Or maybe you're already married and have a kid or two running around the house. Suddenly, your dream of becoming a mom feels less like a dream come true and more like the daily grind of changing stinky diapers, making endless meals, and just keeping your small humans alive. You look at the lives of your unmarried family members and friends and feel a seed of bitterness growing toward their "freedom and independence." Sister, this is right where God wants to meet you.

Or maybe your season of life hasn't fully reached adulting yet. Your best friend seems to have everything (I mean *everything*) that you long for. Even though she's your good friend, you feel resentment and jealousy building up in your heart toward her. You're struggling to congratulate her or rejoice with her in anything. You'd rather grumble about her in your heart and complain to God about how unfair life is. Sister, this is right where God wants to meet you.

Regardless of the season of life you're in or what losses and struggles you're facing, God wants each one of us to choose the path of humility and grace toward others. Choosing to embrace this perspective changed everything for me. When I was tempted to run in the other direction, I asked God to give me a heart of love and generosity toward my sister. And he did. He gave me what I needed for each new hurdle I came upon. And He wants to do that for you too. One day at a time. One step at a time.

His Grace Is Always Sufficient

Okay, full disclosure here. Walking this path of rejoicing with others while simultaneously enduring our own challenges or losses is hard. Like capital H-A-R-D, hard. And it's okay to acknowledge that.

For me, one of the hardest things I faced during this entire season of weeping and rejoicing was Bethany's first baby shower. Everything about this party was a blend of joy and sorrow for me. Everything reminded me that I wasn't pregnant. I had to fight for joy in this moment. I had to counsel my heart and emotions with God's truth. I had to literally put one foot in front of the other. I prayed for God's strength and His perspective.

As hard as that day was, God's grace was sufficient. Second Corinthians 12:9 proved to be true: "My grace is sufficient for you, for my power is made perfect in weakness." I was genuinely able to rejoice with my sister. I was able to celebrate the unique and special plan that God had for her life and the life of her baby. I even helped host the shower. I made quiche, brought a gift, and prayed for the meal. I didn't run away and hide but showed up for my sister and celebrated this special moment in her life.

A few days later, I decided to share about this experience online. I knew others would be climbing a similar mountain and might need some real-time encouragement. I posted a sweet photo of Bethany and me at her shower, along with this:

Celebrated this beauty today. If you had asked me 10 years ago what I thought my future would look like, I definitely would have painted a very different picture than what my reality is today. I grew up always assuming I would get married young, have kids pretty quickly, and live out my days in the sunshine right next to my really hot husband.

Well . . . the first and last dreams came true. ;)

But the middle one . . . wow. That has been an unexpected and challenging journey. I never imagined I would be celebrating the pregnancy of my close sister with nothing to show for myself except loss and heartbreak. I never imagined it. I never hoped for it. But God ordained it. And He never makes mistakes.

What has been even more unexpected than my journey through infertility, is the mysterious way God has synchronized my inner longings to make peace with my outer reality. His grace is truly a sweet and precious gift. He has opened my eyes to see the beauty of His unique plan for each person's life. Just like no two fingerprints are exactly the same, no two life stories are exactly the same. God's sovereign hand directs our paths and leads us down the road he has ordained for us.

Sometimes it's a valley. Sometimes it's a mountaintop. But no matter where the journey takes us, He is always by our side. He is always dispensing fresh grace for each new turn. And because of this, I was genuinely able to celebrate my sister's pregnancy today and praise the Lord for what He's doing in her life. God is good, and He does good.

And who knows . . . maybe one day we'll get to be moms side by side. That would be pretty sweet. But if that dream never becomes a reality, I know God's grace will be sufficient for every step of that journey too. His faithfulness in my life yesterday reminds me to trust Him for whatever He has planned for tomorrow.[2]

Friend, when we fully trust God to write His story for our lives, we can look around and genuinely celebrate what He is doing in the lives of those around us. It is possible for you and me to love others well as we grieve our own losses. And not only is it possible, it's powerful. It's a real-life testimony of the gospel lived out. It's a miracle of grace that God produces in our hearts. There is always room for more. As we choose to live our lives with an outward-focused gaze, we will see how beautiful the world can truly be.

As this chapter comes to a close, I want to ask you a personal question. Has God been stirring something in your heart? Is there someone in your life that you've been ignoring or avoiding? Who do you need to take intentional steps toward in order to celebrate with them? Who do you need to rejoice with? Who has God put in your life for you to love wholeheartedly right now?

Remember, it is more blessed to give than to receive.

When it comes to your unique life story, you don't have to compare and despair. But rather, you can choose to joyfully celebrate the gifts and blessings that God gives to others. It is possible to rejoice and weep at the same time. You can harmonize the two. Sometimes you laugh, sometimes you cry. Your valleys and mountaintops are both beautiful parts of God's greater and grander plan.

Ponder IT

When you fully trust God to write His story for your life, you can look around and genuinely celebrate the good He's doing in the lives of those around you.

Remember

✴ We must learn how to weep over our losses in healthy ways while also rejoicing with the people we love.

✴ With Christ's strength, we can embrace our own seasons of disappointment while simultaneously celebrating with those who receive the very blessings we desire.

✴ It is more blessed to give than to receive.

✴ When we choose to love others when everything in us is screaming to shut down, hide, and retreat, we display a compelling picture of sacrificial love.

✴ It is possible to rejoice and weep at the same time. We can harmonize the two.

SHARE **YOUR HEART**

Dear Lord,

As I wrestle with my own losses and longings, I confess that I don't want to celebrate with others in my life. This is so hard. I'd rather retreat, hide, and ignore what's going on around me. But I know that's not Your way. You are calling me to love others selflessly, and I want that. Help me to become the type of woman who reaches out to her friends and cherishes her family. Give me the grace to process my own losses while keeping my eyes open to what You're doing in other people's lives. I want to become someone who celebrates Your work in other people's lives. I know that it's more blessed to give than to receive. Help me to live this out today.

Amen.

Consider

1 John 4:7-12

Beloved, let us love one another, for love is from God, and whoever loves has been born of God and knows God. Anyone who does not love does not know God, because God is love. In this the love of God was made manifest among us, that God sent his only Son into the world, so that we might live through him. In this is love, not that we have loved God but that he loved us and sent his Son to be the propitiation for our sins. Beloved, if God so loved us, we also ought to love one another. No one has ever seen God; if we love one another, God abides in us and his love is perfected in us.

DEEPER

Isaiah 40:21-31   2 Corinthians 4:16-18

Romans 12:9-21   1 John 4:13-21

WHAT **ABOUT YOU?**

1. When was the last time you had a full-blown ugly cry? What was it about?

2. Why do you think it's so hard to celebrate with people who receive the very blessings you want?

3. What do you find most challenging about rejoicing with those who rejoice and weeping with those who weep?

4. How have you personally experienced the blessing of giving?

5. In what ways do you need to become a better *celebrator* and *rejoicer* of those in your life?

Go **FOR IT**   Regardless of whether you're currently in a season of rejoicing or weeping, who can you intentionally celebrate today? Think of one person right now and write their name on this line: _____. Now, think of one special way you can celebrate this person today (e.g., send them a fun card, call them, buy them a sweet gift, etc.). Write exactly what you're going to do on this line:

_____

Finally, take this step of action to celebrate this specific person within the next twenty-four hours. Ready? Go!

Rejoice with those who rejoice, weep with those who weep.

Romans 12:15

chapter 10

When Life Throws
You a Detour

Have you and Zack thought any more about adoption?" Bethany asked me from across the table. It was Monday morning, and the two of us, along with our sister Rebekah, were out for a fun Girl Defined team breakfast.

"We haven't really talked about it recently," I replied, taking a bite of warm, gooey waffles.

This wasn't the first time the topic of adoption had come up. Zack and I had discussed adoption a lot over the years, but the timing never seemed right. The green light never seemed to be there. We had prayed about it many times but never felt a peace to move forward. Since I had been really public with my journey of infertility, the adoption question came up all the time. *Have you considered adoption? Why won't you adopt? Adoption is a great option!*

"To be honest," I said, glancing at Bethany and Rebekah, "I'm just not sure adoption is the right path for us."

"What makes you say that?" Bethany asked with a smile, genuinely wanting to know.

"Well, I don't know . . . it's just so complicated. And expensive . . . and there are so many unanswered questions. I know it's a beautiful thing and all . . . but I'm just not sure it's the right path for us."

And then, out of nowhere, in the middle of the restaurant, Bethany burst into tears.

I was stunned. *Was it something I said?*

Rebekah glanced at me with huge questioning eyes.

What is happening?

"I'm so, so sorry," Bethany said quietly through her tears. "I don't know why I'm crying. I've just been thinking a lot about orphans lately and how they're so vulnerable and helpless. I'm not trying to pressure you into anything at all. Truly. It just makes me sad thinking about it."

And then, without warning, I suddenly burst into tears too.

Rebekah was doubly stunned. What in the world was happening to her two older sisters? Surely they were past the hamster and vacuum cleaner stage?!

Imagine the scene: Three sisters sitting at a table, two of the three crying. For no apparent reason. I'm sure the waiter was avoiding us.

"I don't know why I'm crying too!" I said while dabbing my face with a napkin. "I just feel so unsure about the future. I don't know what to do."

Rebekah glanced at me with understanding eyes while Bethany wiped some dripping mascara from her cheek.

"And to be totally transparent," I continued, "the thought of adoption really scares me. There are just so many unexpected issues and potential challenges."

Pushing her plate of bacon and eggs aside, Bethany looked across the table with compassionate eyes and asked me a question that would ultimately set my life on a new course. "Do you think *fear* is the deeper reason you're hesitant to consider adoption?"

The world froze. My thoughts swirled around me in slow motion. Deep in my heart, I knew the answer to her question.

Yes.

I was completely terrified.

This unexpected and tearful conversation over waffles and eggs exposed something deep in my heart. *I was gripped by fear of the unknown.*

Remember, I'm the girl who likes to do things inside the box. I prefer a safe, risk-free life, with all my ducks neatly in a row.

Adoption is the opposite of that.

That's why it scared me so much. There were so many question marks surrounding the entire process. So many hurdles. It was easier to just ignore it and explore other opportunities. But God was stirring something in my heart.

I went home that day, determined to get to the bottom of my fear. I searched the internet for any helpful books on adoption. Maybe I needed to start growing in my understanding of what the Bible says about adoption. I quickly came across a book called *Adopted for Life: The Priority of Adoption for Christian Families and Churches* by Russell Moore. I purchased the audiobook version and began listening to it right away. I felt desperate to learn and grow.

I wanted to discover more of what God's heart is for adoption. I wanted to gain more of a gospel perspective and framework.

I popped in my earbuds, turned on the audiobook, and headed to my backyard to get some work done. Multitasking while listening to audiobooks is a must for me. I had been on a power-washing kick, so I turned on the sprayer and got to work. (Quick side confession: I'm addicted to power washing now. It's one of the most rewarding and fulfilling projects you can do. Seriously, just try it. Your life will be changed.)

So, there I was, power washing my back patio while listening to *Adopted for Life*. Over the next few hours, with mud and water all over me, God did a transformational work in my heart. The compelling words of Russell Moore opened my eyes to see adoption in a whole new light. He talked about the parallels that adoption has with the gospel. How adoption is one of the most beautiful pictures we have of what God has done for us. Just as Christ came to our world, rescued us, renamed us, and adopted us into His own family, we have the opportunity to do the same for others. As we fight for orphans, bring them into our families, and give them our own name, we mirror our great Redeemer. We rescue the vulnerable, just as Christ has rescued us.

My heart was softening.

The gripping fear that had resided in me for far too long was slowly being replaced by something more powerful. *Love.* As 1 John 4:18 says, "There is no fear in love, but perfect love casts out fear." As the day went on, the fear I had carried around for many years was completely gone. This was nothing short of an act of God. My heart was being transformed by the beauty of the gospel in a whole new way.

I'm the orphan who has been rescued and adopted by Jesus. Thank You, Lord!

As I continued power washing, the author said something next that stopped me dead in my tracks. It went something like this: Do you desire most to get pregnant, or do you desire most to be a mom? Because if you desire most to be a mom, adoption is a beautiful opportunity.

Wow.

Tears filled my eyes. I had been holding on to my dreams of getting pregnant for so many years that I couldn't see beyond them. I hadn't made room in my heart for God to show me a different path. To me, starting a family had always meant birthing biological children. But what if God had a different plan? As the power washer continued to blast my patio, I prayed a silent prayer of surrender. *Lord, if You want us to adopt, please guide us down the right path. Show us what to do. My heart is wide open. Lead me wherever You want.*

> The gripping *fear* that had resided in me for far too long was slowly being replaced by something more powerful. *Love.*

Over the next few weeks, Zack listened to the same audiobook that I had listened to and was just as impacted by it as I was. We began praying about adoption together in a more fervent and focused way. We asked our families to pray with us. We researched dozens of articles, podcasts, and videos online about adoption. As our understanding grew, our hearts grew with it. After a few months, the direction was crystal clear.

We were going to adopt.

My heart was bursting with joy as we told our closest friends and family members. I couldn't believe this was happening.

Over the next few weeks, we felt led to adopt internationally and chose an adoption agency to help us. After learning more about the many orphans in Ukraine, we looked into that country and felt very drawn to it. We also had some personal family and friend connections to Ukraine, so our hearts were already fond of it. God was clearly directing our steps.

The most exciting part, though, was when Zack and I both discovered we were open to adopting more than one child. We were standing in our kitchen one morning when I casually tossed out the idea to Zack.

"What do you think about adopting more than one child?" I held my breath.

Zack looked at me and said, "Honestly, I was thinking about the same thing!"

Wow. Only God.

As we learned about the many orphaned sibling groups in Ukraine, our hearts were moved with compassion and love for them. We told our agency that we were open and excited to adopt two or even three siblings.

The Lord works in mysterious ways!

We didn't waste any time finding an agency and getting started on the paperwork. We quickly began chipping away at the home study, the educational training, the government forms, and more. The stack never seemed to go away . . . until it finally did. Six months later, we joyfully shipped our entire dossier (i.e., massive stack of notarized forms) over to Ukraine. Then we waited. But we didn't have to wait long. Less than two months later, we got an unexpected call from our agency saying that Ukraine had processed our entire dossier and approved us for adoption from their country.

We were ecstatic!

Then, just a few weeks later, we received our official invitation and appointment from the Ukrainian government to travel to their country. Two weeks later, we were flying across the Atlantic to be matched with our future children.

One thing that is somewhat unique about the Ukrainian adoption process is that they don't give you a referral for a child/children until you're actually present in their country at your appointment. So Zack and I had zero clue as to who we would actually be adopting. Talk about nerve-racking!

Thankfully, our jitters were calmed as we reminded ourselves of how God's hand had so clearly been in every part of our adoption process. We could trust His leading. We were confident He would unite us with the children that He had ordained for our family.

And He did.

On February 25, 2021, we were matched with two precious brothers, ages ten and six.

I'll never forget the moment I met them for the first time at their orphanage. Without hesitation, they ran straight over to Zack and me and greeted us with the most enthusiastic joy and smiles. My fears of wondering if I would "connect" with them vanished the minute they wrapped their little arms around me in a big hug. I was toast!

We spent two wonderful days with them, just hanging out and getting to know one another. Even though they only spoke Russian and we only spoke English, we got pretty good at hand gestures and facial expressions. We had a wonderful time and some good laughs.

The hardest part was leaving. Ukraine's process requires a bunch of additional paperwork to be filed after the match takes place. So, we flew back to Texas to patiently await our second invitation.

Then, four weeks later, we were back on a plane to finally pick up our boys in Ukraine.

Standing before a Ukrainian judge with our children standing next to us, we spoke the words that would legalize the adoption forever. One moment they were orphans, and the next moment they were our sons.

What a breathtaking picture of the gospel.

Bringing them back home to America was one of the sweetest memories of my life, and I will cherish it forever. They're home. And I truly love these boys more than life itself. God is so good. What a gift.

As I survey the landscape of my life today (LEGOs and Nerf gun bullets all over my floor), I can't help but smile.

A God-Ordained Detour

Zack and I didn't set out to write our story this way. This isn't the life we'd originally dreamed of, but it's better than anything we could have imagined. The reality of going from zero kids to two makes Zack and me laugh and shake our heads in amazement. Our families playfully joke with us about how it's finally time we're experiencing sticky little fingers on our white walls and gum on our car seats. Zack is still adamant about not allowing food in his truck . . . but we'll see how long that lasts.

In the midst of this beautiful but crazy change in life direction, I came across a powerful quote by Elisabeth Elliot that deeply resonated with me. She said,

Some of God's greatest mercies are in His refusals.[1]

Sometimes God says no to one thing so He can say yes to something else—something you can't even see on your horizon, something you can't even imagine.

I don't know about you, but in this life, I often view closed doors and detours as negative things. When our prayers seemingly go unanswered or when opportunities pass us by, it's natural to view this as a problem and an upset to our plans. Have you ever felt

> Sometimes God says *no* to one thing so He can say *yes* to something else.

that way? But what if God is doing something bigger in the "refusals"? What if God is saying no to something now because He wants to say yes to something later?

As I thought about this more, I realized I had fallen into a trap that a lot of women fall into. I had been viewing the closed doors and detours in my life story as second-best options. In my mind, the ultimate bull's-eye was to get married, have biological kids, and live a perfect little life with a happily-ever-after bow on top. That was my goal. So when my story took some unexpected turns, I subconsciously viewed them as roadblocks to my dreams. They were obstacles that stood in the way of my future. They were annoying detours that kept me from reaching my greatest destination.

But what if this route wasn't a detour?

What if your current life route isn't a detour?

What if this route is actually God's best path for your life?

What if *this journey* is the life God is calling you to live for His glory?

As I pondered these questions myself, a lightbulb went on.

I realized that I had been struggling to fully embrace God's story for my life because I was viewing everything through the lens of "what should have been." *My life should have turned out this way. My life should look different. My life should be further along.* Ever felt that way? But the reality is, we're not holding the pen to our life story. God is. And the story we've always imagined isn't necessarily the one He planned for us. Romans 11:33 reminds us that God's ways truly are mysterious: "Oh, the depth of the riches and wisdom and knowledge of God! How unsearchable are his judgments and how inscrutable his ways!"

My life wasn't falling off the tracks; it was right on God's track. And yours is too.

Over the years, I've watched so many women fall into the same trap I fell into. Their lives weren't turning out the way they'd expected, and they were struggling to truly thrive in their reality. Singleness was lasting a lot longer for one friend, so she viewed that season of her life as a waiting zone. Another friend's dream of serving as a missionary overseas fell through, so she viewed her life as spiritually purposeless. Another friend lost one of her parents to cancer, so she viewed her life as half-empty.

These losses and disappointments are extremely hard, but what if God is weaving these hard seasons into a beautiful tapestry that's bigger than what you can see? What if these detours to your plan are a part of God's greater plan for your life?

As you look at your own life, what roadblocks have you seen? What unexpected twists and turns has your life taken?

Embracing God's Plan

As I've wrestled with this in my own life, I've realized that fear and pride were at the root of my resistance toward God's story for me. I was afraid of the unknown future, and I was too prideful to surrender my plans to God. If you find yourself in a similar place of resistance, I want to share a few biblical truths that greatly helped me on this journey. God used these truths to change my heart and open my hands to the new direction He had for me. Maybe they're just what your heart needs too. In order to fully embrace God's unexpected plan for our lives, we have to get a few things right.

I. Get humble before God.

Humbling ourselves before God is a foundational part of the Christian life. It's a heart posture that says, *God, You know better than I do. May Your will be done in my life.* As the well-known "Lord's Prayer" from Matthew 6 teaches us to pray, "Your kingdom come, your will be done" (v. 10). This is a prayer of humble surrender to God. We must open our clenched fists and release the story of our lives into God's sovereign care. We must humble ourselves before Him and acknowledge that He knows best.

2. Choose trust over fear.

When we fear our life circumstances, we're not fully trusting God. But when we fully trust God, we will no longer fear our circumstances. Proverbs 29:25 says, "The fear of man lays a snare, but whoever trusts in the LORD is safe." When we're led by fear, it becomes a crippling snare in our lives. It hinders us from wholeheartedly following God. But when we choose to trust God fully, we find safety. We're empowered by Him to step forward confidently in faith, knowing He is with us.

3. Follow His direction.

Following God is easy when He leads us where we want to go. But what about when He leads us where we don't want to go? This is where faith comes in. By faith, we follow God's leading in our lives, even when we don't have all the answers. We might not have all of our ducks in a row yet. And that's okay. God does. By faith, we take one step at a time, trusting that He will give us what we need for the direction in which He is leading us. As Psalm 37:23 reminds us, "The steps of a man are established by the LORD, when he delights in his way."

Detours to our life dreams and plans are hard, but when we humble ourselves, choose trust over fear, and follow God by faith, we can step forward confidently. The future may be unknown to us, but it's very clear to Him. Detours don't have to be detrimental.

As we look throughout the Bible, we see detour after detour in the lives of so many women. One of the most unexpected detours was probably one that happened in the life of Mary, the mother of Jesus. As a young woman engaged to her fiancé, Joseph, she probably imagined her life turning out pretty normal.

But it didn't.

Out of nowhere, an angel of the Lord visited her and said she was going to supernaturally conceive and give birth to the Savior of the world.

Ummm, say what?!

Talk about a detour! But how did Mary respond? She didn't get angry at God for disrupting her plans and dreams. She didn't allow fear to overwhelm her emotions. She didn't demand a five-year plan. Instead, she chose to humble herself under God's sovereign hand and say, "Behold, I am the servant of the Lord; let it be to me according to your word" (Luke 1:38).

That, right there, is what it means to accept God's unexpected detour for your life.

Mary's humble response is a powerful testimony to us as modern women today. She was probably a teen girl, and yet her faith and trust were anchored in the Lord. She embraced God's detour and trusted Him with the outcome of her life.

God is calling us to trust Him in the same way.

As I type these words right now, Zack and I are literally in the middle of trying to figure out how to be parents to our two growing and energetic boys. I'll let you in on a little secret. I don't know what I'm doing! But thankfully, I have a lot of support. As I sit in my backyard, watching my boys run around the yard with the dog, I am amazed at God's grace and kindness to bless me with such sweet gifts.

God always had a plan. It was just different from mine. And I'm so grateful for that. As Proverbs 19:21 regularly reminds me, "Many are the plans in the mind of a man, but it is the purpose of the LORD that will stand."

Sister, God is always working, even when you can't see it. He is weaving together the good, bad, hard, and beautiful parts of your story for a greater purpose. I never imagined that God would use my miscarriages and longings for motherhood to lead me down the path of international adoption.

But He did. He saw the beginning from the end, and He had a plan. He is doing the same thing in your life too. He is working. Choose to follow Him. Choose to trust Him. Choose to love Him.

May we be a generation of modern Christian women who courageously trust God to write our life stories as we join hands and say,

Behold, I am the servant of the Lord; let it be to me according to your word. (Luke 1:38)

Ponder IT

God is always working, even when you can't see it. He is weaving together the good, bad, hard, and beautiful parts of your story for a greater purpose.

Remember

★ Your life story is in the hands of the Creator of this world.

★ God sees the beginning from the end and is working all things for your good and His glory.

★ What if God is saying no to something now because He wants to say yes to something later?

★ Let's join Mary in saying, "Behold, I am the servant of the Lord; let it be to me according to your word."

SHARE YOUR HEART

Dear Lord,

I need You. Oh, how I need You. I am weak and quick to get mad when life doesn't turn out the way I expected. I confess that it's really hard for me to trust You with the direction of my future. You see my dreams and longings, and I know Your timing is perfect . . . but I struggle to embrace Your plan. Help me. Strengthen me. Cultivate in me a humble heart like Mary's, one that is quick to accept Your will for my life. Help me to embrace the life You have for me right now instead of waiting for a different season to come. You are a loving Father, and Your plan is much greater than mine! Thank You for caring about my life. Help me to see the unique ways I can serve You and build Your kingdom today.

Amen.

Consider

Luke 1:26–38

In the sixth month the angel Gabriel was sent from God to a city of Galilee named Nazareth, to a virgin betrothed to a man whose name was Joseph, of the house of David. And the virgin's name was Mary. And he came to her and said, "Greetings, O favored one, the Lord is with you!" But she was greatly troubled at the saying, and tried to discern what sort of greeting this might be. And the angel said to her, "Do not be afraid, Mary, for you have found favor with God. And behold, you will conceive in your womb and bear a son, and you shall call his name Jesus. He will be great and will be called the Son of the Most High. And the Lord God will give to him the throne of his father David, and he will reign over the house of Jacob forever, and of his kingdom there will be no end."

And Mary said to the angel, "How will this be, since I am a virgin?"

And the angel answered her, "The Holy Spirit will come upon you, and the power of the Most High will overshadow you; therefore the child to be born will be called holy—the Son of God. And behold, your relative Elizabeth in her old age has also conceived a son, and this is the sixth month with her who was called barren. For nothing will be impossible with God." And Mary said, "Behold, I am the servant of the Lord; let it be to me according to your word." And the angel departed from her.

Job 40:1-24	Psalm 91:1-16
Psalm 20:7	Jeremiah 17:7-8

WHAT **ABOUT** YOU?

1. How would you respond if an angel suddenly appeared to you, like Mary, with life-altering news about your future?

2. What unexpected twists and turns has your life taken so far (even small ones)?

3. In what ways do you find yourself struggling to embrace certain parts of your life story because you thought it would turn out differently?

4. What did you find encouraging about Mary's humble response in Luke 1:38?

5. What's one area of your life story that you need to fully surrender and entrust to God?

Go FOR IT Grab a piece of paper and a pen. Draw a straight line down the middle of your paper. On the top of the left side, write "Longings," and on the top of the right side, write "Opportunities." Now, starting with the left side, take a few minutes to brainstorm and write down every unfulfilled longing that you have right now (e.g., more friends, boyfriend, marriage, job, better health, etc.). Next, on the right side of the paper, write down every blessing and opportunity that you have right now (e.g., friends, health, ability to learn, God's Word, etc.).

Finally, spend a few minutes praying over each side of your list. For the left side, pray and ask God to give you a heart of trust and surrender in each of those areas. For the right side, thank God for each of the blessings and opportunities you have, and ask Him to help you fully embrace those things right now.

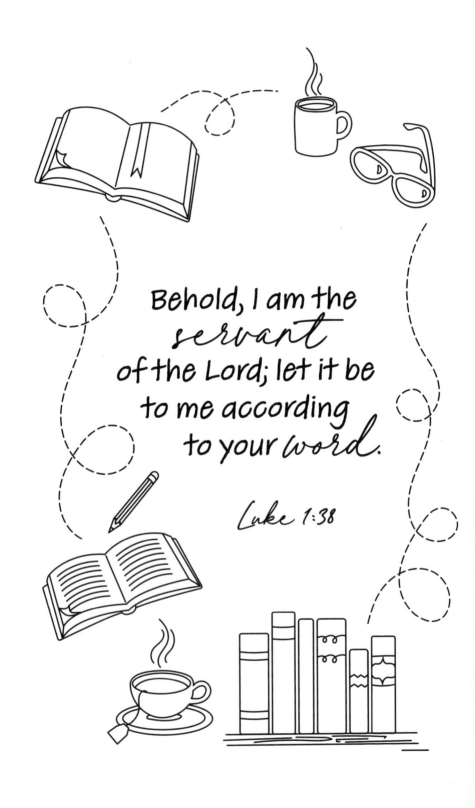

Behold, I am the *servant* of the Lord; let it be to me according to your *word.*

Luke 1:38

chapter 11

Seeing the Beauty in Your Story

t was a picture-perfect Valentine's Day. I (Bethany) had everything my heart desired and then some. I walked hand in hand with my handsome husband into the candlelit steak house. The waiter escorted us to our corner booth. We sat down and just stared at each other. Both of us knew what was coming. I looked at my husband with nervous anticipation and said, "This is it! This is our last Valentine's Day with just the two of us. Next year our sweet little baby, Davey Jr., will be with us! Our family is about to change forever."

Little did we know that our family was about to change very soon. Like this-very-night soon.

Despite the fact that I was nine months pregnant and felt like a beached whale, we enjoyed every minute of our romantic evening out. We reminisced about our wedding day. We laughed about how nervous we had been on our very first date. And we were amazed by all that God had done in our short year and a half of marriage. God had blessed us with each other, and that was more than either of us could have asked for. God sure knew what He was doing when He wrote our life stories. His plan for us was so much better than the story we would have written if we'd had control of the pen.

We left the restaurant full and happy.

The rest of the evening was ours to enjoy. We had ice cream waiting in our freezer and gifts wrapped and ready to go. We pulled out of the restaurant and headed toward our place. As we were driving, my belly started to ache a little. I felt different. *This can't be it*, I thought. *I'm sure it's just Braxton Hicks contractions. I'm sure there's nothing to worry about.*

The moment we arrived home, a full-blown contraction hit me. Maybe the steak launched me into labor? I looked at David with a look that only a very pregnant wife on the verge of going into labor can give her husband.

He knew.

I didn't say a thing.

The next hour consisted of me trying to distract myself and David nervously timing contractions. Things seemed to be progressing extremely fast, especially considering this was my first time giving birth. I'd heard that the first birth can be slow. Whatever was going on inside me didn't feel slow. We agreed that David should call the midwife and get her opinion. Our midwife listened carefully to everything I had to say. She said to call her back in an hour with an update.

The next hour flew by. The contractions were progressing rapidly. David hopped on the phone and gave my midwife another update. The entire time he was on the phone, I kept telling myself that I was probably being dramatic. I'd heard over and over again that first-time moms are often anxious and mistake strong Braxton Hicks contractions for real ones. My midwife knew better. She packed her bags and headed out. She was at our place with her team in under thirty minutes.

My midwife's arrival brought a huge sense of peace. The professionals were here, and I could rest knowing they were ready to help me have my dream labor and delivery in the comfort of my very own home. Without hesitation the midwives jumped into action. They immediately examined me to check my progress.

After a few minutes of assessing the situation, my midwife gave me the best news in the entire world. "Girlfriend, you are eight centimeters dilated. You're having a baby tonight!"

Oh, the relief that came over my heart. This was it. I was about to meet my sweet baby boy.

From that moment on, my labor progressed full speed ahead.

After two more hours of intense contractions, I pushed out the most beautiful baby boy I'd ever laid eyes on. He was precious. David and I leaned back together on our bed with sweet, little Davey Jr. in our arms. The labor was done. Our baby was here. Davey Jr. was the best Valentine's Day gift we could have ever asked for.

And then day two of motherhood hit.

I've often heard it said that the first twelve weeks of your baby's life are considered your fourth trimester. I didn't fully understand what that meant until I went through it. Labor and delivery ended up being the easy part.

Postpartum wrecked me. Physically and emotionally.

I was the biggest hot mess you'd ever seen. Postpartum hormones are no joke. Praise the Lord, I had a loving husband and an amazing family who were there with me every step of the way. Every latte delivered was like Christmas morning.

The next few months after Davey's birth proved to be some of the hardest months of my entire life. I experienced more physical pain and recovery issues than I ever knew were possible. My trust in God was tested in huge ways. I wondered if life would ever feel bright and cheery again. I wondered if my body would ever heal. I wondered if Davey Jr. would ever latch on and nurse. I wondered if I'd be attached to a breast pump for the rest of forever. I wondered if I'd ever be able to use the restroom without experiencing excruciating pain (hemorrhoids, anyone?). I wondered if I'd ever sleep again.

Throughout that fourth trimester, God was doing a work in my heart. He retaught me the same lessons He'd been teaching me throughout my entire life. Just as He was faithful in my singleness, He would be faithful in these early days of motherhood.

Not gonna lie though, the temptation to compare my life— my mothering skills, my postpartum progress, my body— with other moms' was ten-out-of-ten hard. It seemed like there was a specific standard for new moms, and I often felt like I was a total failure. I wasn't even close to measuring up to the "ideal" standard of motherhood I saw on social media.

I remember one particular instance of comparison that left me especially disheartened. It was after another tried-and-failed attempt at breastfeeding. I decided to text a few different friends to ask about their experiences. I remember feeling discouraged as I compared every little detail of my difficult experience to their seemingly smooth journeys. It seemed as though everywhere I turned, there was someone or some article telling me the correct way to do things. The correct way to be a mom.

In those moments of comparison and worry, my sweet husband gently reminded me to keep my eyes up and on my Savior. This new season of life wasn't about winning a mom prize or doing better than anyone else. It wasn't about comparing my circumstances to those of my friends, my sisters, or strangers online. God wasn't calling me to live anyone else's life. He was calling me to run in my lane and live my life for His glory. He's given me my husband and son for a reason. He doesn't want me to compare but to pour out my life and to love those around me.

He was reminding me to look straight ahead and focus on Him instead of looking to my left or to my right.

Girlfriend, Let's Ditch Comparison

I'll be the first to admit that I am a gold prize winner at this whole comparison game. I have four sisters and several sisters-in-law, so there is endless room to compare. Each one of us has our own unique personality, gifts, talents, strengths, and weaknesses. Not to mention all the physical differences. We're all entering different stages of life, going through different highs and lows, and experiencing different milestones.

Kristen and I are the closest in age (less than two years apart), which makes the comparison trap all the more prevalent. As you've already read in previous chapters, we've both been through seasons in which we each had the very thing the other wanted. Kristen got married; I remained single. I got married and had a baby; Kristen remained without a baby. Talk about the perfect comparison storm.

Did we struggle with comparison? Absolutely.

Did we struggle with jealousy? You bet.

Did we struggle with anger? Yes.

Although we've both struggled in different ways and at different times, the answer to overcoming the comparison trap has always been the same. *Trust God, and pour out your life for others.* The more we each focused on loving and serving others, the less we struggled with comparison. The more we accepted God's unique path for our lives, the more we stayed in the lane God had for us.

I'm sure you've had, or have, your own comparison trap. Maybe it's with a sister or a cousin or a friend. Maybe you're tempted to compare yourself with that flawless social media influencer. Or maybe it's with that successful coworker who constantly seems to be two steps ahead of you. (*Can't she just quit already?*) None of us can escape the fact that there will always be people around us living the life we desire. Which means there will always be opportunities for comparison.

Thankfully, success (according to the Bible) isn't about competing with those around us. It's not about comparing and feeling proud that we're better than the sister next to us. Not at all. The Christian life is about running the *individual* race God has set before us.

Therefore, since we are surrounded by so great a cloud of witnesses, let us also lay aside every weight, and sin which clings so closely, and let us run with endurance the race that is set before us, looking to Jesus, the founder and perfecter of our faith, who for the joy that was set before him endured the cross, despising the shame, and is seated at the right hand of the throne of God. (Heb. 12:1–3)

Do you see the words in the very middle of the passage? "*Looking to Jesus* . . ."

That's it. That is the key to defeating comparison. It's running the race God has set before *you*. Not the race He's set before your sister, your coworker, or your bestie. It's *looking to Jesus* and remembering that He is your reason for life. Jesus set this example for us by coming to earth and living out His purpose. He went to the cross because He knew that was the calling God had for Him. He ran the race set before Him and kept His eyes on God. He is the perfect example of what it means to run the race set before us.

Whenever the two of us (Kristen and Bethany) find ourselves struggling with comparison, we slow down and remember Jesus's example. He ran the race set before Him and never compared. We need to do the same. The more we keep our eyes on Him, the more we will faithfully embrace the unique journey He has for us.

Here's another thing: we're not each other's competition. *Say it loud for the sister in the back!* Girl, we're not designed to fight against each other. We are, as 1 Corinthians 12 describes, the body of Christ. We're each uniquely gifted to love and serve in different ways. You know the analogy. What good would a body be if every part wanted to be the eye or the leg or the toe or the belly button (outie or innie)? The body wouldn't be a body; it would just be that one part. Talk about a useless body if every part were the big toe. No offense to big toes.

You are your own unique aspect of the body of Christ. God wants to use you to bring glory to Him in ways that your friend can't. In ways that your sister can't. He is calling you to love people in ways unique to only you.

> God wants to use you to bring *glory* to Him in ways that your friend can't.

When our eyes are on Jesus, there is no room for comparison.

The two of us thought it would be really encouraging to give you an inside peek into the lives of our three younger sisters. No two stories are the same. From ours to theirs, it's clear that God has a unique plan for each of our lives. Over the years, it's been so neat to celebrate our differences and cheer each other on. We're each other's literal sisterhood. Instead of comparing and fighting against each other, we choose to celebrate and enjoy the unique journeys God has us on.

Ellissa's Story

Our sister Ellissa is six years younger than Kristen and four years younger than me. When we were all in our preteens and teens, the age gap felt like an eternity. Now it feels like nothing.

Ellissa has always had a heart for missions. For as long as we can remember, she's had a passion for orphans, China, and reaching the lost with the good news of Jesus. God has used those unique passions in Ellissa's life to do some incredible things. After Ellissa graduated from high school, she had the opportunity to spend several summers in China serving in orphan care. Her love and passion for those orphans will impact those sweet kids for years to come. And God will continue to use the investment she's made in ways she'll never know this side of heaven.

But Ellissa never could have imagined what God was going to do with her life next.

She had absolutely no idea that God was preparing an amazing Ukrainian man to be her future husband—but that's what happened. Through the mission branch of her church, Ellissa met a godly and dashing young man named Andrii. What seemed like an impossible circumstance turned into a beautiful long-distance dating relationship. Though the challenges of living thousands of miles apart and having major cultural differences and language barriers certainly existed, the two of them persisted. Dating eventually turned into engagement, and engagement eventually turned into marriage. Our sweet younger sister now lives in Ukraine alongside her husband, Andrii. They spend their days as full-time missionaries, loving the people of Ukraine and ministering wherever they can.

What a story. And it's only just begun.

Do you think that Ellissa would have ever written this story for her life? No way. Marrying a man from Ukraine and moving halfway across the world weren't part of her plan. She probably never imagined she'd have future children (Lord willing) who would grow up speaking Ukrainian. Thankfully, Ellissa chose to look to Jesus and trust Him. She put Proverbs 3:5–6 into action and allowed God to direct her path. Was it scary at times? Oh yes. Worth it? One hundred and fifty million percent.

God's not done with Ellissa's story either. He has a unique race set before her and Andrii. The two of us are excited to cheer our sister on and celebrate the beautiful journey God has called her to walk.

Rebekah's Story

Rebekah is our sweet, curly-haired little sis. She's twelve years younger than Kristen and ten years younger than me. Although the two of us are more than a decade older than Rebekah, we've maintained an incredibly close friendship. We've loved watching her grow up and blossom into a beautiful young woman.

Rebekah is the go-getter, an organized, you-can-count-on-her-to-get-the-job-done kind of girl. Over the past several years, she's chosen to spend her time investing in the next generation. Although she was only a teenager herself when she started mentoring younger women, she didn't let her young age stop her from pursuing discipleship opportunities. She kept her eyes on Jesus and was committed to fully living right where God had her. She's always been the kind of girl who exemplifies 1 Timothy 4:12, which says, "Let no one despise you for your youth, but set the believers an example in speech, in conduct, in love, in faith, in purity."

While Rebekah was taking college classes, she decided to use what little free time she had left to volunteer for Girl Defined Ministries as an intern. She did whatever work needed to be done (which was oftentimes not glamorous. Packing and shipping, anyone?). After she graduated from college, she officially started working for the ministry as a full-blown team member. Over the past few years, she's taken on the role of conference coordinator, shop manager, donor relations director, and more. She's risen to the challenge and trusted God for the grace and strength to do the job well. She's chosen not to compare her life to those around her and instead focuses on running the race God has set before her.

If you've ever wondered if God can use a young woman to make a big impact, Rebekah's story is proof of that. Allow her story to inspire you to keep your eyes on Jesus and to faithfully run the race before you.

Suzanna's Story

The sweet baby of our family. That's right. Suzanna is the little (okay, not so little at five foot eleven) baby of the fam. She's the most vivacious, joyful, expressive, life-of-the-party kind of girl you will ever meet. She is confetti wrapped up in a person. If you're ever feeling down, just invite Sue over and you'll be smiling in no time.

Sue is the type of girl who pours her heart into everything she does. If she invites friends over, she makes them feel super loved. If she's working on an art project, she gives it 110 percent. Whatever she decides to do, she does it well. Sue has also been blessed with pretty much all of the artistic talent in our family. She can paint or draw the most beautiful and detailed pictures. Instead of only using her talents for personal advancement, though, Sue has chosen to use her talents to serve others. She's blessed so many people with custom family portraits, insanely pretty birthday banners, and hand-painted cards.

There is no doubt that God has amazing works in store for her. Kristen and I can't wait to see what God does with her talents. Oh, and did we mention that she has also joined the team at Girl Defined Ministries? She's our lead designer and social media manager, which is pretty impressive considering she's only a teenager and has just barely graduated from high school. She has been a major blessing to the ministry. Her spiritual encouragement through artwork has reached thousands of girls from around the world. She has a gift that keeps on giving.

Sue is an inspiration. She focuses on using her life to glorify God and invests her talents in serving people. She strives to run her race and keeps her eyes on Jesus. How cool is that? We think it's pretty awesome for a teen girl.

Your Story

This is your spot. This is your story. If I (Bethany) were to type out what you've done with your life up to this point, what would I type? Would I be able to say that you've chosen to run the race God has set before you and are using your time, talents, and energy for His glory? Would I be able to say that you are looking to Jesus? That you're not comparing your life with those around you but are thriving in the one life God has given you?

If you're anything like me, this is probably an area of struggle for you. Especially considering the highly media-driven world we live in today. It's so easy to get on social media and compare ourselves with the "highlights" from thousands of people's lives around the world. We can compare ourselves to the most famous movie stars and the most popular workout gurus. To the trendiest fashionistas and the wealthiest women. The list of people we can follow and compare our lives to is endless.

As I continue on my journey of motherhood, I must remind myself that it's not a competition. I've personally found myself having to be uberintentional to steer clear of this comparison trap. Entering the world of motherhood has presented endless possibilities for this. If I'm not extremely careful in this area, I'll end up in a pit of despair because my life doesn't seem as perfect as what I see online.

I've personally found that I need to be extra cautious with what I allow into my life. Instead of watching the latest shows, listening to whatever is most popular, and following whoever's trending, I need to make sure I'm only allowing things into my life that help me run this race well. If I'm allowing things into my life that are constantly tempting me to compare, that's probably not the best idea.

I'm sure you can relate.

When we stop looking to our left or to our right (whether in real life or online) and instead keep our eyes on Jesus, we're better able to run the race God's set before us. You're not called to run my race. You're not called to run Kristen's race or one of our sisters' races or anyone else's race. God is calling you to run your race.

That's it. He will equip you with the strength you need for every step of the way.

> God is calling *you* to run your race.

The two of us are so grateful that God doesn't treat life as if it were some sort of worldwide Olympic Games. He doesn't line us up in different events and make us compete. God doesn't pit us against one another to battle for the gold medal. He's actually doing the opposite. He's given us the sisterhood from around the world (all of us who are believers in Jesus) to cheer each other on. We're supposed to be here for each other. To support each other. To love each other. To celebrate with each other. To make each other stronger. To use our unique gifts and talents to build up the body of Christ.

Let's cheer for the sisterhood.

When you look to your left and see a sister do something awesome, cheer her on. When you look to your right and see a sister get an amazing blessing, cheer her on. When your friend goes on that date with an amazing guy while you're still single, celebrate that joy with her. When your coworker gets that promotion you've been hoping for, be the first to congratulate her. When your mom-friend posts photos of the week-long vacation she went on with her husband, ask her questions about how it went and what her favorite part was.

Look for opportunities to cheer your sisters on as you run your race.

We're all in different places in life. Maybe you're a teenager trying to pass your next class, or a college graduate trying to secure your first job, or a twentysomething praying that God will bring you a husband, or a newlywed figuring out how to love your husband, or a married woman hoping to have children, or a mom just trying to survive the next day. Wherever you are right now, God wants you to focus on Him as you live each day for His glory alone.

Don't allow comparison to cripple you from living the life God has right in front of you. You can rest knowing that God is sovereign. Choose to run your race for His glory. *He is worthy.*

Ponder IT

You can rest knowing that God is sovereign. He is working to help you run your race well. Keep your eyes focused on Him. *Look to Jesus.*

Remember

★ The Bible makes it very clear that success isn't about competing with those around us but serving God wholeheartedly.

★ Life is about running the race God has set before us as individuals. It's an *individual race*, not a group competition.

★ The more we keep our eyes on Him, the more we run faithfully in our lane in the race God's called us to.

★ When our eyes are on Jesus, there is no room for comparison.

★ God is calling you to run your race. He will equip you with the strength needed for every step of the way.

★ Let's look for opportunities to cheer each other on as we run our race.

SHARE **YOUR HEART**

Dear Lord,

I know You say to keep my eyes on You. I know that's the answer to overcoming the comparison trap. But it's hard. It's hard when I'm seeing all of the "highlights" on social media. It's hard when my friends seem to be getting everything that I so desperately want. Help me to run my race. Help me to run in my own lane and to focus on living for You. Help me to pour out my life for others and serve those around me. Help me to celebrate my sisters and friends rather than compare. Change the desires of my heart so that I'll be most concerned about glorifying You. I want to live for You.

Amen.

Consider

──── **Galatians 5:13-14** ────

For you were called to freedom, brothers. Only do not use your freedom as an opportunity for the flesh, but through love serve one another. For the whole law is fulfilled in one word: "You shall love your neighbor as yourself."

──── **Philippians 2:1-11** ────

So if there is any encouragement in Christ, any comfort from love, any participation in the Spirit, any affection and sympathy, complete my joy by being of the same mind, having the same love, being in full accord and of one mind. Do nothing from selfish ambition or conceit, but in humility count others more significant than yourselves. Let each of you look not only to his own interests, but also to the interests of others. Have this mind among yourselves, which is yours in Christ Jesus, who, though he was in the form of God, did not count equality with God a thing to be grasped, but emptied himself, by taking the form of a servant, being born in the likeness of men. And being found in human form, he humbled himself by becoming obedient to the point of death, even death on a cross. Therefore God has highly exalted him and bestowed on him the name that is above every name, so that at the name of Jesus every knee should bow, in heaven and on earth and under the earth, and every tongue confess that Jesus Christ is Lord, to the glory of God the Father.

Matthew 5:16	Ephesians 2:10
Romans 12:9-13	Hebrews 12:1-3
Galatians 6:9	1 Peter 4:10-11

WHAT ABOUT YOU?

1. Is there someone in your life who has set a great example for cheering others on?

2. In what ways do you compare yourself with those around you?

3. In what ways has social media made the comparison trap more difficult for you?

4. How does "looking to Jesus" free us from comparison?

5. Why is it important to run our own race and not the races of those around us?

6. How might God want to use your unique journey to bring glory to Himself?

Go **FOR IT**   Grab a piece of paper and write "My Story" at the top of the page. Underneath that, write three or four sentences describing the highlights of your life journey up until this point. Next, write "Five Years from Now." Underneath that, write three or four sentences about ways you hope to run in your lane and serve Jesus over the next five years. Begin praying that God will use you to live for Him and that He'll make the next five years of your life all about bringing Him glory.

Let us run with *endurance* the race that is set before us, looking to Jesus, the founder and *perfecter* of our faith.

Hebrews 12:1-2

chapter 12

Looking for Kingdom Moments

Can you believe it's been almost ten years since you got married?" I said to Kristen from the passenger seat of her car. The two of us were on our way to prep for an upcoming speaking engagement. As usual, we were using the drive time to catch up on life.

"It's crazy!" Kristen responded. "Some days it feels like our wedding was a lifetime ago, and other days it feels like it was yesterday." She paused for a moment, then said, "It's so weird. My life today isn't at all what I imagined it would be ten years ago."

"Right?" I agreed. "Same goes for me."

"Speaking of weddings," Kristen continued, "whatever in the world happened to that crazy wedding dress you bought?

Not the dress you wore for your actual wedding but that other one. The super-sparkly princess-looking thing."

We both laughed.

I hadn't thought about that dress in a very long time. It had been hanging in the back of my closet for so long that I'd almost forgotten it was still there. Although it had been my dream dress when I bought it, it wasn't my dream dress when I got married (almost ten years later). I just couldn't picture myself walking down the aisle to my husband in a Cinderella explosion. It wasn't me anymore. Lesson learned. Don't buy your wedding dress until you have sights on the groom.

When my wedding did eventually roll around, I decided to count my losses and buy a different dress that better represented my current style preferences.

With all these memories flooding my mind, I looked at Kristen with an embarrassed smile and said. "Oh my goodness. That dress! Yeah . . . so, you're not going to believe this. That huge white dress is *still* sitting in the back of my closet. I still have it."

Kristen burst into laughter. "What?! Who does that? Who pays over a thousand dollars for a dress and then never actually wears it?"

I guess spontaneous, outside-the-box, crazy girls like me do that.

Maybe one day I'll find a sweet bride who's dreamed of wearing a dress exactly like that one. I've been looking for her! Until then, the dress will probably continue to hang in the back of my closet and take up much-needed space. My poor husband is losing closet space to a wife who wants to store not one but two wedding dresses. He sure got a catch when he married me.

When Kristen and I think back on the past decade of our lives, we smile, because some things never change. Like the wedding dress still sitting unworn in my closet. But on the other hand, some things have changed a lot. Like the fact that we're both married women, watching our little families grow in unique and beautiful ways.

Looking back over the past decade, we can't help but be in awe of the journey God has taken us on. We have learned that no matter where the road leads, we will thrive if our focus is on Christ and if our goal is to build His kingdom.

And that's ultimately the story of this book.

It's about a God who loves His children enough to lead them, guide them, and use them for His glory. God has a unique plan for each of our lives. A plan that is different from what any of us would've imagined but much more beautiful in the end. A plan that includes mountaintop moments and seasons in the dark valleys. A plan that ultimately paints a picture showcasing the incredible talent of the Artist who painted it.

> God has a *unique* plan for each of our lives.

The Bigger Picture

Let's revisit a few of the highlights we've learned throughout our time together.

One: The more you get to know God's character, the more confident you will be to trust Him with your unknown future.

Two: Whether or not God ever gives you the longings of your heart, you can find lasting peace and fulfillment in your relationship with Christ.

Three: Choosing not to worry doesn't mean that you don't care about the problem; it means you take your problem to God and trust Him with the outcome.

Four: True joy and real suffering can coexist.

Five: God isn't some sort of distant deity who's detached from human experiences and pain but an intimate, relational, and loving Father who walks with His children through their suffering.

Six: Filtering your emotions with truth doesn't mean you ignore your feelings; it means you bring God into your feelings.

Seven: God is the Master Painter. One day you will be able to look back and see the beautiful masterpiece He painted with your life for His glory.

Eight: The surrendered life is focused on serving God throughout every season.

Nine: When you fully trust God to write His story for your life, you can look around and genuinely celebrate the good He's doing in the lives of those around you.

Ten: God is always working, even when you can't see it. He is weaving together the good, bad, hard, and beautiful parts of your story for a greater purpose.

Eleven: You can rest knowing that God is sovereign. He is working to help you run your race well. Keep your eyes focused on Him. *Look to Jesus.*

If you remember only one thing when you finish this book, we hope it's this: Never buy a wedding dress until you have a ring on your finger.

Just kidding.

Although, that's not terrible advice.

Seriously though.

The one thing we hope you'll take away from this book comes from some of the most important words Jesus left us with. You may recognize this passage because it's commonly known as the Great Commission.

And Jesus came and said to them, "All authority in heaven and on earth has been given to me. Go therefore and make disciples of all nations, baptizing them in the name of the Father and of the Son and of the Holy Spirit, teaching them to observe all that I have commanded you. And behold, I am with you always, to the end of the age." (Matt. 28:18–20)

That's it. Right there. That's what life is ultimately about. It's about building God's kingdom and making His name great. It's not about building our own little kingdoms with our perfect families and white picket fences. It's not about building a social media following that attracts brand deals. It's not about being the most liked, respected, or admired gal. It's not about having your dream life come true.

It's about so much more than that.

And the "so much more" part is where true joy and hope are found.

The two of us have found over and over again that the more we desire God's kingdom, the more our earthly priorities align with kingdom priorities. We've found that true peace and contentment come when we're focused on living for our King.

True *peace* and contentment come when we're *focused* on living for our King.

Focusing on building God's kingdom is the very reason we've been able to thrive in the midst of our own unfulfilled longings. When I (Kristen) came face-to-face with the reality that I may never carry a child full term, I had to remind myself that even in the midst of my pain, God was sovereignly fulfilling His good purposes in my life (Ps. 138:8). This truth enabled me to continue using my life to love and serve. Because of my kingdom mission, my life had purpose, even when I didn't understand what God was doing.

When I (Bethany) wondered why I was single for many years longer than I'd ever hoped or imagined, I'd remind myself that my life purpose was about glorifying God. That was my reason for existing. If God wanted me to do that as a married woman, He would provide a man. If He wanted me to do that as a single woman, I would remain single. By embracing my ultimate life purpose in each season, I was able to truly thrive.

Looking for Kingdom Moments

Since the core purpose of our lives is to glorify God and build His kingdom, how do we do it? Is it mainly about restraining from yelling at someone who rudely and unashamedly says you're "freakishly tall"? We're not talking about containing your crazy emotions the next time you give away your beloved hamster either. Although, you better believe we're never buying hamsters again.

So, what does it mean to build God's kingdom?

It's actually very simple. It's changing the lens through which you look at life. It's viewing life through a lens that says, "How can I point someone to Jesus today?" It's looking for those little moments to make His name great. Kingdom moments could look like any of the following:

Responding with kindness and grace when someone makes a mean comment about you in person or online. Showing them the love of Jesus in spite of their actions.

Choosing to celebrate the engagement of your best friend while you're still desperately praying for a man of your own. Putting Romans 12:15 into action.

Taking that first step toward your difficult coworker and inviting her out to lunch . . . and paying if you can afford to.

Pursuing reconciliation with your difficult in-laws and showing them Christ-centered sacrificial love. Even when you feel like they're in the wrong and you're in the right.

Making the time to pray for that unsaved family and proactively sharing the gospel of Jesus with them.

Choosing to forgo the new summer wardrobe in order to support an orphan living thousands of miles away.

Getting outside your comfort zone and willingly volunteering to serve at church in whatever ways are most needed.

Praying and asking God to use you in whatever way He sees fit.

There are endless opportunities to go after kingdom moments. It just takes a willingness to put yourself second and God first. It means taking your eyes off of what you want out of life and focusing instead on what God wants from your life.

Sister, we want you to look back a decade from now with such joy and gladness over the way you've chosen to live. We want you to experience the fullness of life that comes only from living to glorify God. We want you to look back with peace, knowing that you entrusted your future to God and handed Him the paintbrush to your story.

Take a moment right now to slow down and talk to your amazing Father. Use the words of Psalm 138 to ask God to fulfill His good purpose in your life.

> I give you thanks, O LORD, with my whole heart;
>> before the gods I sing your praise;
> I bow down toward your holy temple
>> and give thanks to your name for your steadfast
>> love and your faithfulness,
>> for you have exalted above all things
>> your name and your word.
> On the day I called, you answered me;
>> my strength of soul you increased.
>
> All the kings of the earth shall give you thanks,
>> O LORD,
>> for they have heard the words of your mouth,
> and they shall sing of the ways of the LORD,
>> for great is the glory of the LORD.
> For though the LORD is high, he regards the lowly,
>> but the haughty he knows from afar.
>
> Though I walk in the midst of trouble,
>> you preserve my life;
> you stretch out your hand against the wrath of my
>> enemies,
>> and your right hand delivers me.
> The LORD will fulfill his purpose for me;
>> your steadfast love, O LORD, endures forever.
>> Do not forsake the work of your hands.

The picture God is painting of your life is still in process. It's not over yet. There are still deep valleys and high mountaintops ahead. The road will curve, twist, and take unexpected turns. You may find yourself in a dark forest or in a sunlit field. Wherever God leads you, remember that it's not about getting to the peak but about faithfully walking the journey.

Give your loving Savior the paintbrush.

He wants to do far more with your life than you ever imagined possible.

When your hope is found in Jesus, you will thrive. As you look ahead and wonder what will be next, rest knowing that God holds your future. He will be there with you. No matter where the journey takes you.

The Story Isn't Over

The two of us thought it would be cool to share a current life update with you. Y'know, one of those "So, where are they today?" kinds of things.

I (Kristen) am loving our new life as a family of four. I still can't believe it. Every time one of my sons calls me "Mama," it melts my heart on the spot. Zack and I are helping our boys chip away at their English lessons while also having a blast sharing some of our favorite hobbies and activities with them (camping, anyone?). Each day is filled with joys and challenges, which keep me reliant on Christ. And yes, Zack finally let the boys bring food in his truck.

I (Bethany) am in full-time mom mode. Davey Jr. is full of energy and on the go. I love him more than life itself. I often catch myself just staring at him in amazement. One of those "How is this my life?" sort of looks. He's just the best thing ever. David and I would love to give Davey a few younger siblings if God allows. We like the idea of having a houseful of children. And maybe a dog too. David and I are still talking about that one. Kids, yes. Dog, maybe. We will see.

Kristen and I would love your prayers as we continue trusting God and surrendering every day of our lives to Him. We'll be praying for you. Who knows? Maybe we'll write a "Part 2" book in another decade or so, sharing about the many ways God continued to work in our lives.

Until then, we plan to enjoy the journey. We're praying you will too. Sister, let's cheer each other on. Every twist and turn along the way.

Ponder IT

> Life is ultimately all about building God's kingdom and living to make His name great.

Remember

* God has a magnificent plan for each of our lives. A plan that is different from what any of us would've imagined but much more beautiful.

* Ultimately our greatest purpose in life is to build His kingdom.

- ✴ If the ultimate aim of our life is anything other than Jesus, we've missed the point. We've missed our calling.

- ✴ He is the very reason we exist. He is the reason we live. He is the reason we have hope.

- ✴ We want you to experience the fullness of life that comes from living to glorify God.

- ✴ Open up your hands. Give your loving Savior the paintbrush. He wants to do far more with your life than you ever imagined possible.

SHARE YOUR HEART

We've written out a prayer for you in each of the past eleven chapters. It's your turn now. We want you to write your own prayer this time. Take a few minutes to grab your journal and write out your prayer to God.

Consider

──────── **Matthew 28:16-20** ────────

Now the eleven disciples went to Galilee, to the mountain to which Jesus had directed them. And when they saw him they worshiped him, but some doubted. And Jesus came and said to them, "All authority in heaven and on earth has been given to me. Go therefore and make disciples of all nations, baptizing them in the name of the Father and of the Son and of the Holy Spirit, teaching them to observe all that I have commanded you. And behold, I am with you always, to the end of the age."

Revelation 4:11

Worthy are you, our Lord and God,
>to receive glory and honor and power,
for you created all things,
>and by your will they existed and were created.

DEEPER

Psalm 90:2	John 5:24
Psalm 102:25-27	John 14:6
Psalm 145	Revelation 4

WHAT **ABOUT YOU?**

1. What's something you did over a decade ago that's still a vivid memory?

2. Look back through the highlights listed from chapters 1-12. Which of those stood out to you most and why?

3. How should the Great Commission impact your daily life?

4. How can you go about building God's kingdom instead of your own?

5. How is it possible to thrive when life doesn't go according to your plan?

Go **FOR IT**   It's time to look for a kingdom moment. Grab five or six sticky notes and a pen. Write the words "kingdom moment" on every single sticky note. Stick the notes all over your bathroom mirror. For the next several days, allow these notes to remind you to look for kingdom moments. Every time you find yourself doing something that is "Kingdom Moment" worthy, pull a sticky note off the mirror and use the back to write out what you did. Continue doing this until all the sticky notes are pulled off the mirror.

Go
therefore
and make
disciples
of all nations.

Matthew 28:19

ACKNOWLEDGMENTS

God . . . thank You, first and foremost, for giving us the opportunity to write this book and for showing us Your incredible faithfulness through the ups and downs of life.

Zack and Dāv . . . our biggest fans. Thank you for being there for us, yet again! You never seem to grow weary of cheering us on, and we are grateful for that.

Our awesome families . . . thanks for always being there for us during each book-writing endeavor. Your prayers, words of encouragement, and overall interest in our books always give us the boost we need.

Rebekah Guzman . . . thank you for believing in us (again) and giving us the opportunity to write this book. We can't thank you enough!

Patti Brinks . . . this cover is beautifully unique, and we love it. Thank you for working with us to create something outside the box for this special book. You are the best.

Baker Books . . . your team is incredible. We have truly loved working with every single person at Baker. Thank you for partnering with us to publish *Not Part of the Plan*.

Friends who supported us along the way . . . thanks for sticking with us through yet another book. We're grateful for you!

NOTES

Chapter 1 When Dreams Don't Come True

1. Timothy Keller (@timkellernyc), Twitter, November 10, 2014, 3:31 p.m., https://twitter.com/timkellernyc/status/531906966550228993?lang=en.

Chapter 2 This Isn't What I Wanted

1. Nancy Leigh DeMoss (Wolgemuth), Revive Our Hearts, Facebook, September 20, 2013, https://www.facebook.com/ReviveOurHearts/posts /anything-that-makes-me-need-god-is-a-blessing-we-want-to-be-confi dent-strong-and/10151852400664437/.

Chapter 4 The Bright Side of Disappointment

1. Kaitlin Miller, "Why Would God Allow My Disappointment?," *Desiring God* (blog), November 23, 2020, https://www.desiringgod.org /articles/why-would-god-allow-my-disappointment/.

2. David Murray, "Six Steps Out of Disappointment," Desiring God, accessed January 6, 2021, https://www.desiringgod.org/articles/six-steps -out-of-disappointment.

Chapter 6 Hello, Crazy-Girl Emotions

1. Erin Davis, "10 Powerful Truths to Counteract Deceptive Emotions," *Lies Young Women Believe* (blog), February 3, 2009, https:// liesyoungwomenbelieve.com/10-powerful-truths-to-counteract-deceptive -emotions/.

Chapter 8 Freed Up to Live for Him

1. Nancy Demoss Wolgemuth, "Betty Scott Stam: A Life of Surrender," *True Woman* (blog), accessed May 6, 2021, https://www.reviveour hearts.com/true-woman-/blog/betty-scott-stam-life-surrender/.

Chapter 9 Sometimes You Laugh, Sometimes You Cry

1. Kristen Clark (@krstnclark), Instagram post, August 15, 2019, https://www.instagram.com/p/B1M3LhlH-mz/?igshid=1uh63qb9p4wcr.
2. Kristen Clark (@krstnclark), Instagram post, February 1, 2020, https://www.instagram.com/p/B8CfofEHAWj/?igshid=1luohmbd0lesv.

Chapter 10 When Life Throws You a Detour

1. Elisabeth Elliot, "The Prayer of Faith: God's Refusals are His Mercies," on *Gateway to Joy* (radio program), June 13, 1989, accessed January 6, 2021, https://elisabethelliot.org/resource-library/gateway-to-joy /the-prayer-of-faith-gods-refusals-are-his-mercies/.

ABOUT THE AUTHORS

Kristen Clark is married to her best friend, Zack, is the mom to two energetic boys, and is cofounder of Girl Defined Ministries. She is passionate about promoting the message of God-defined womanhood through blogging, speaking, mentoring young women, and hosting Bible studies in her living room. In the end, she's just a fun-lovin' Texas girl who adores all things outdoors and drinks coffee whenever possible.

Bethany Beal is head-over-heels in love with her best friend and husband, David, and is the super-proud mommy of Davey Jr. She is cofounder of Girl Defined Ministries and is passionate about spreading the truth of biblical womanhood through writing, speaking, and mentoring young women. To her family and close friends, she is simply a tall blonde girl who is obsessed with iced lattes and can't get enough of her sweet baby, Davey Jr.

Kristen and Bethany are the authors of *Girl Defined*; *Love Defined*; *Sex, Purity, and the Longings of a Girl's Heart*; and *Shine Bright*.

ALSO AVAILABLE FROM
KRISTEN *&* BETHANY!

In a culture where airbrushed models and ultra-driven career women define beauty and success, it's no wonder we have a distorted view of femininity. *Girl Defined* offers a distinctly God-centered view of beauty, femininity, and self-worth. Based firmly in God's design for our lives, this book invites us on a liberating journey toward a radically better vision for femininity—one that ends with the kind of hope, purpose, and fulfillment we've been yearning for.

DISCOVER GOD'S BEST FOR
your romantic
relationships

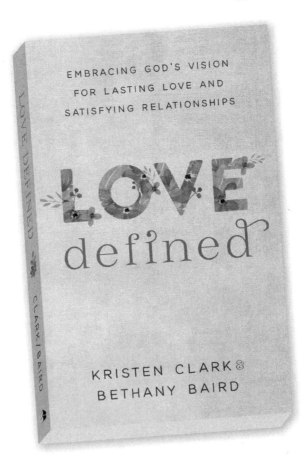

Covering topics such as true love, purposeful relationships, sex, boundaries, and singleness, *Love Defined* will take you on a journey to discover God's good and original design for romance.

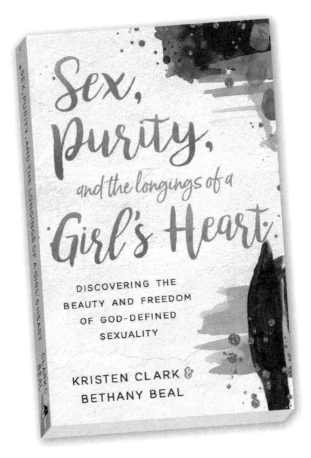

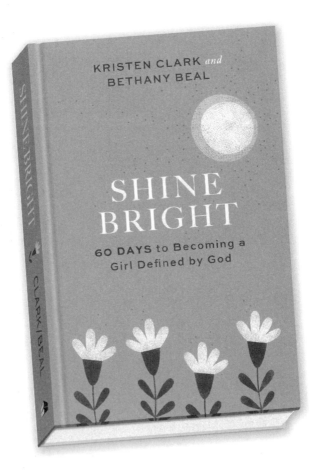

Girl Defined
MINISTRIES

Continue learning about
God's *incredible design*
for women . . .

GIRLDEFINED.COM

Listen to their new podcast,
The Girl Defined Show

▶ Girl Defined	🐦 Girl_Defined
📷 GirlDefined	📌 Girl Defined
f GirlDefined	✉ contact@girldefined.com

FOLLOW
Bethany and Kristen
ON SOCIAL MEDIA!

bethany.beal

bethany@girldefined.com

krstnclark

kristen@girldefined.com